Buckets and Brawn

The History of Sarasota
and Its Fire Department

by Wayne A. Welsh

"We Serve with Excellence and Pride"

DEDICATION

To my wife Debi and daughter Amy who give meaning to everything I do.

"Greater love has no one than this, that one lay down his life for his friends."
John 15:13

Printed in the United States of America
1993
First Edition

Published by Wayne A. Welsh

Library of Congress Catalog Card Number: 93-061202

Hardcover ISBN 0-9638831-0-0
Paperback ISBN 0-9638831-1-9

COVER PHOTO: Firefighters enter a pool of burning fuel under the protection of a hoseline to attempt a daring rescue.
Photo by Suzanne Friend Whelan.

Contents

ACKNOWLEDGMENTS

The writing of *Buckets and Brawn* was a seven year journey that was filled with surprises and discoveries. During this journey, I encountered a multitude of delightful individuals who shared a common love for history. It has been my pleasure to associate with each of them and to transform their photographs and memories into *Buckets and Brawn*. I value their friendship and will always have a warm place in my heart for them. I am indebted to Patrick B. Whelan who painstakenly edited and unquestionably improved this work. I can never express how fortunate I am to have such a loving and patient wife and daughter. Thank you Debi and Amy for your patience and the cups of hot tea on those late nights. I am grateful to those individuals and organizations listed below for their assistance in the writing of *Buckets and Brawn*.

INDIVIDUALS

Lillian Burns
Gene Cobb
Mrs. James R. Cowsert
Helen Caravelli
Bill Carlin
Francis Currin
George I. (Pete) Esthus
Lucille Hayes Everett
Gregg Faegans
Thomas Fields
Oliver K. Fletcher
Alice Titus Franklin
James L. Frazier
Elbert E. Friend
Tate Gabbert

Pam Gibson
Julius E. Halas
Dr. J.D. Hamel, Chaplain
Vince Hernandez
Robert Horne
Bonnie Johnson
Grace Knowles
James Knowles
Maitland Knowles, Jr.
Jeff LaHurd
Eula Lastinger
Miles Lawrence
Dan Lestz
Nina Lewis
Rotha Harvey Matson

Janet Snyder Matthews
John McCarthy
Nathalie McCulloch
Judy McCloud
Hap McNeely
Gordon Norman
Joanna Norman
Ron Norman
Jim Olson
Deanna Osborn
Ambrose Petellat
Charlotte V. Roberts
Whit Rylee
Dennis Sargent
Dr. Linda Schlumbrecht

Francis Scott
Ann A. Shank
Harold Stinchcomb
Yvonne Thomas
Dorothy Tuynman
Bob Viol
Amy Lynne Welsh
Debi Friend Welsh
Josephine Wensel
Patsy West
John J. Whelan, Jr.
Patrick B. Whelan
Suzanne Friend Whelan

ORGANIZATIONS

The Bradenton Herald
City of Sarasota Fire-Rescue
Florida Photographic Collection-Bureau of Archives and Records
Historical Society of Sarasota County
Manatee County Historical Society
Manatee County Library-Eaton Florida History Room
National Hurricane Center, National Weather Service, Coral Gables, Florida
News Center Channel 40-WWSB
Sarasota County Central Records
Sarasota County Department of Historical Resources
Sarasota Herald Tribune
Sarasota-Manatee Professional Firefighters and Paramedics- Local 2546

SPONSORS

The following corporate sponsors have demonstrated their concern for a fire-safe community through their financial contributions to *Buckets and Brawn*. Their generous donations have made *Buckets and Brawn* a reality. These organizations which have demonstrated their dedication to the preservation of life and property continue to be leaders in the community. Their willingness to give to the community of which they are so vital a part is sincerely appreciated.

Associates In Internal Medicine
P. Burt Veazey, M.D.
Brad S. Lerner, M.D.
Lydia G. Corn, M.D.
Robert L. Oppenheimer, M.D.
Bernard J. Feinberg, M.D.

Coastal Printing, Inc.

Historical Society of Sarasota County

Lancet Technology, Inc.

Les King Fire and Safety Equipment, Inc. (Since 1954)

Norton Camera & Video

Ringling School of Art and Design

Sarasota Lock and Key

Specialty Gloves & Dental

Suncoast Fire and Safety Equipment

PREFACE

Buckets and Brawn is a memorial to those unselfish individuals, both past and present, who battle one of nature's fiercest forces: FIRE. As a trumpet boldly resounds its message, this book declares the brave heritage of those individuals with the fortitude to endure the fight.

The firefighters of the City of Sarasota Fire Department have shown unselfish dedication to the preservation of life and property for over 80 years. They potentially risk their lives every day they report for duty. Yet, these knights in shining armor are just regular people. They are husbands and wives, fathers and mothers, sons and daughters, who feel elation when a life is saved and share a family's grief when a life is lost. They confront danger with gallant effort because they feel that they can make a difference. Firefighters touch the hearts and lives of our community.

Writing a history book about firefighters is much like being a detective. One must tediously search for clues that when pieced together tell the story of years past. These clues often surface in attics, family photo albums, newspapers, and municipal records. Regrettably, records are often lost or destroyed to the detriment of writers and historians. Fire, age, neglect, and even the acid of the paper destroy some. Others are not recognized for their inherent value and are discarded. The most enlightening truths are preserved in the consciousness of those individuals who were present when the events of bygone days unfolded. Their memories vividly recall the sights and sounds of times past with a realism that historical documents can never match. Time erases memories while nature destroys the written record.

People knowledgeable with Sarasota's past will find portions of this book familiar. But just as a portrait would not be complete with parts of its subject missing, this book would not paint the entire picture of the Sarasota Fire Department if portions were omitted merely because the information had previously appeared in other publications. Readers will walk chronologically through the challenges faced by the developing department and will see how Sarasota's fire department was indeed built by buckets and brawn.

Diligence has paid off, the results of which you now hold in your hand. This book is an attempt to share with present and future generations the colorful history of the City of Sarasota Fire Department. Theirs is a proud heritage!

CHAPTER 1

A PLACE TO CALL HOME

"Nature, in order to prove her art, made one bay more beautiful than any other; where the skies shine bluer and the sunsets are more gorgeous; where fruits grow sweeter and the perfume of flowers is more fragrant; where warm Gulf breezes caress more tenderly in winter and Ocean's breath is cooler in summer; where the songs of birds swell with a finer melody; where the spirit of Man can almost span the gap as he contemplates her handiwork. Nature has proved her Art — WE HAVE SARASOTA."[1]

Sarasota's first settler, William Henry Whitaker, arrived in Sarasota Bay on December 14, 1842. Traveling with his half-brother, a Tallahassee lawyer named Hamlin Valentine Snell, he packed his small sailing vessel with supplies and sailed southward. William previously had labored as a fisherman for five years and had an opportunity to examine the coast closely. His favorite spot became Sarasota Bay. By 1843, before Florida was even a state, William had saved enough money to buy land warrants for the purchase of public lands around Sarasota Bay. Upon arrival in the area, William was drawn to the tall yellow bluffs from his days as a fisherman. The distinctive bluffs were mounds of oyster shells, bones, and other discarded materials from the tribes of Indians that had inhabited the same site. The "Yellow Bluffs" as they were called were located just south of a bayou, now called Whitaker's Bayou, on the east bank of which flowed a crystal-clear spring. With his arrival at Yellow Bluffs, William knew that he was home. He may have felt that he had indeed found a bay more beautiful than any other.[2]

Yet Whitaker's home was in a frontier wilderness. Many of the hardships that he experienced in building a home, family, and even a town were common to many pioneers throughout American history. Those who desired to enjoy the beauty and bounty that Sarasota offered during the first decades also endured Indians, war, mosquitoes, alligators, and perhaps above all the perils of fire.

Whitaker's first order of business was to construct two temporary lean-tos from palmetto logs, one for provisions and one for shelter. In 1843 Whitaker decided to build his first permanent home, which he built from cedar logs that he floated from Longboat Key. The Whitaker home was typical of many of the early homesteads. Sturdy cedar logs with ends that fitted together formed the exterior walls. A privy stood outside — at a reasonable distance from the house, of course. Wood shake shingles covered the roof and helped protect the inhabitants from the torrential summer rains. In addition to rain, the summer also brought with it heat and humidity. During the winter the fireplace served for cooking the plentiful fish and wild game and for warming the house. During the hot summer, however, the cooking and baking was done outside in a detached kitchen. The detached kitchen helped to distant the fire threat from the house. Having a fire inside in the subtropical climate would make temperatures almost unbearable. Outdoor cooking was usually done over an open hearth made of stone.[3,4]

Most early homes had a shaded porch in order to

take advantage of the tropical gulf breeze. Houses were also built with the floor level several feet above the ground to protect them from flooding during the rainy season. But the elevated floors that helped with flooding caused problems with vermin for Sarasota's pioneers. One early pioneer said, "Pigs could and did

powerless to stop them. Since flames often raged through the palmettos within close vicinity of the homes, burning embers ignited the thatch that had accumulated on the rooftops. The homes, along with the hopes and dreams of the owners, were frequently destroyed by the flames.

Mary Jane Wyatt Whitaker and Bill Whitaker confronted Indians, Union soldiers, hurricanes, and fire while homesteading in beautiful Sarasota.

COURTESY SARASOTA COUNTY DEPARTMENT OF HISTORICAL RESOURCES

get under our house and fleas developed by the million. Nearly ate us up! Pops sprinkled wet salt under, but finally got some alligator hides and put under and soon the fleas disappeared."[5]

During the cold season, it was not uncommon for a harmless "coach whip" snake to make his way into the house and stretch out on the open rafters since early homes were constructed without ceilings. The unwelcome guest would promptly be shooed down and out the door.[6]

The construction features of the early homes predisposed them to the ever present threat of fire. Settlers painstakingly cut small clearings in the dense vegetation to provide just enough space for their homes. The result was a wood house located in the midst of a multitude of trees, palmetto and other underbrush. The dense vegetation regularly burned, especially in the summer, because of the hot conditions and lightning.

The uneven surfaces of the wood shingles caused them to catch and hold falling pine needles and, unfortunately, flying embers created by the seasonal brush fires. When fires occurred, the owner was generally

In 1849 Whitaker met Mary Jane Wyatt. She had lived with her parents Colonel William Wyatt and his wife Nancy on the Manatee River in the Samoset-Oneco vicinity. Her pretty and soft southern ways were sufficient enticement for him to ride the fifteen mile journey to come calling for the next two years during their courtship. Whitaker's frequent visits to the Wyatt household wore a sandy wagon trail, Sarasota's first road. Despite the fact that Mary weighed only 80 pounds and was barely five feet tall, she was a spirited belle. While at her father's ranch, she became an expert at horseback riding, cattle herding, tree-trunk canoe paddling, and shooting. Her father claimed that she could shoot the head from a turkey at a hundred yards.[7,8]

At age 30 Whitaker decided to put an end to the single life and took eighteen year-old Mary for his bride. Their wedding was consecrated in the Methodist church in Manatee County on June 10, 1851. Whitaker proudly took his bride to their new home at Yellow Bluffs, on Sarasota Bay, where they began their family.[9,10]

CHAPTER 2

ON THE WARPATH

Florida was home to the Indians long before whites arrived. The tall yellow bluffs that William Whitaker saw when he first sailed into Sarasota Bay were actually refuse mounds from generations of Indians. After Spain ceded Florida to the United States in 1821, immigrants poured in and demanded possession of the lands. The United States government ignored the Indians' claim to the land and pressured some leaders of the Seminole Tribe to sign a treaty in 1823 that relinquished their land rights to the whites and restricted the tribe to limited reservations. Indian resentment grew when the Florida Legislature drastically reduced the size of the Seminoles' reservation. When the United States finally attempted to relocate the Seminoles to the Indian Territory in Arkansas, the Seminoles refused. Violent skirmishes broke out between the whites and the Seminoles, thus beginning the seven-year Seminole Indian War.[1]

The United States government had devoted nearly 40 million dollars and 3000 lives in the effort to force the Seminoles to emigrate from Florida. Both parties grew weary of the war, which had been characterized by draining hit and run tactics in the thick Florida wilderness. The war ended on August 14, 1842, four months before Whitaker sailed down to Sarasota to start his homestead. The Seminoles agreed to restrict themselves to a reservation for hunting and planting located in the south Florida cypress swamps. Holata Micco, known to the settlers as Billy Bowlegs, was recognized as the head chief of the Seminoles in Florida. In describing his nickname *Harper's Weekly*, like whites generally in the 1840's, regarded the Indians with little respect. "The name 'Bowlegs' did not imply any parenthetical curvature of his lower limbs. Billy's legs were straight as an arrow when he was sober, which is by no means his normal state."[2]

Mary Wyatt Whitaker had a different impression of Billy Bowlegs. She first met him in the summer of 1850 while spending time on her father's ranch. The Indian chief would visit the West Coast often to trade and sometimes to enjoy a meal with the settlers. Mary became well acquainted with Billy and spoke with him on several occasions regarding his tribe. One day Mary boldly asked Billy Bowlegs, "If there should be an uprising of the Indians and massacre, would he kill them." He replied to her surprise, "Yes, they would kill them easy," meaning that the Indians would grant them a swift and painless death rather than the torturous death that other whites might receive.[3,4]

Billy Bowlegs was a proud and stocky man who enjoyed spending time in his banana patch. With banana stalks over fifteen feet tall, pumpkins ripening on the vines, and potatoes in the ground, the banana patch was truly a source of joy to Billy, and he loved to admire its beauty.[5]

The federal government in their effort to put pressure on the Indians ordered a survey of the Big Cypress Swamp. They intended to map the existing Indian villages and trails for information to keep the Indians in check. The Army's assistance was enlisted, and Lieutenant George Hartsoff took his company of ten men from Fort Myers to complete the assignment.

Seminole Indian Chief, Holata Micco in his native regalia. He was known to Florida Settlers as Billy Bowlegs. The two medals upon his chest bear the likeness of Presidents Martin Van Buren and Millard Fillmore.

In December 1855, Hartsoff and his men came upon Billy's prized banana patch. One of the men said, "Let's tear the hell out of it and see what Billy does." The soldiers did just that. This malicious act began a course of events that resulted in the Third Seminole War. When Billy discovered the vandalism that had occurred, he was outraged and soon confronted Hartsoff and his men personally. After ridiculing the Indian chief, they threw him face down on the soil of the banana patch he had loved.[6,7]

Early on Christmas Eve the Seminoles retaliated. Billy returned to the soldiers' camp with a band of Seminole warriors, whose faces were smeared with war paint, and attacked without warning. Moments later, the Indians seriously wounded Hartsoff and four of his men. The remaining soldiers managed to escape, taking their wounded with them. Enraged, the Seminoles broadened the attack by striking out at "the white man's country," shooting, pillaging, and burning white settlements on the coast. The news that the Seminoles were on the warpath sent alarm throughout the coast. Mary Whitaker left Yellow Bluffs and sought refuge with her children in Doctor Branch's fort on the Manatee River whose palmetto log stockade was reinforced to offer greater protection against the oncoming Indian raiders.[8,9,10,11]

While his wife remained in the protection of the fort, William Whitaker departed for the nearest military camp which was located 70 miles away on the Peace River. He arrived after four days of riding through the cypress swamp and told of the Hartsoff attack. As a result of his leadership and experience in fighting Indians, Whitaker was named First Lieutenant of a company of volunteers who vowed to protect their loved ones by driving the enraged Seminoles out of the area.[12,13]

Mary Wyatt Whitaker was an unselfish individual who ministered to the sick and needy, both Indians and whites, throughout Manatee County. She opened her doors often to feed the hungry and care for the sick. One of those infirm individuals whom she cared for was George Owen, a young man struck with tuberculosis. He traveled from Philadelphia to the area hoping that the change in climate would restore his health. This trip earned him the title of "Sarasota's first tourist." Mrs. Whitaker invited Owen to seek refuge from the approaching winter in her home, an offer that he gratefully accepted. Home cooking, a roof over his head, and plenty of Florida sunshine put Owen on the road to recovery. In spite of his infirmities, Owen was a proud and courageous man, and he refused to leave the Whitaker home to take refuge from the Indians. Reluctantly, Mary left him behind when she departed with her children and fled to the safety of the Branch home and fort in Manatee.[14,15]

With many families in the Branch fort, supplies and food dwindled. None of the settlers knew just how long it would take to stabilize the situation with the Indians or how long they would be confined within the walls of the fort. Hance Wyatt, Mrs. Whitaker's brother, volunteered to go to Sarasota to get some potatoes from the Whitaker homestead. Traveling only a portion of the journey, Wyatt stopped to rest and have a smoke. His delay may very well have saved his life. While resting he found tell-tale signs of Indians. A reconnaissance led him to climb the nearest tree. While his arms clung to the tree, Wyatt's eyes riveted on what was occurring in the clearing ahead. He was watching the entire Whitaker home engulfed in fire. The flames danced and the smoke rose skyward, as did the soul of George Owen, who perished in that fire on March 3, 1856. Wyatt had just witnessed Sarasota's first arson fire. Good judgement and common sense convinced Wyatt to return to the fort without delay. He took news of the savage attack with him.[16,17,18]

Government troops and civilian posse progressively closed in on the Seminoles. Billy Bowlegs

This location, once known as the "Yellow Bluffs," is the spot where the Seminole Indians burned the home of William and Mary Wyatt Whitaker.

Bill Whitaker's second home was destroyed by fire in 1926. It was located where 12th Street and U.S. 41 are today. Whitaker built it about 1857 after his previous home at Yellow Bluffs was destroyed in 1856 by fire at the hands of Billy Bowlegs and his tribe.

realized that it was just a matter of time before he and his band of 38 warriors would be defeated. So when the federal government offered to pay Billy and his tribe to immigrate to the Indian Territory in Arkansas, he reluctantly accepted on behalf of his tribe. In May 1858 Billy and his tribe boarded the steamer Grey Cloud, and the settlers breathed a sigh of relief.[19,20]

After the Indian War, Whitaker and many other settlers faced the task of rebuilding their homes, fields, groves, herds, and lives. Mary and William Whitaker returned to Yellow Bluffs and built a new two-story home of fine finished cedar lumber shipped from Cedar Key. The home was located on the east side of what is now Tamiami Trail North and Twelfth Street, just west of the Whitaker Rosemary Cemetery.[21,22]

In their new house the Whitaker family expanded and thrived. Mary's gardens and William's cattle herd grew and prospered during the late 1850's. The future appeared bright until the succession of eleven southern states including Florida led to the War Between the States.[23]

During the Union occupation of coastal Florida, the Whitaker home became a target for numerous bands of marauding Union soldiers. Union soldiers came in 1863 and pillaged the household, confiscating or destroying whatever they desired. The soldiers carried away all edibles including both livestock and garden vegetables.[24,25]

Lillie B. McDuffee details the events that occurred later that year in her book, *The Lures Of Manatee*:

> *"The men, after ransacking the house of all its belongings not too cumbersome to take along, called for matches to set the house on fire. Without arguing, Mrs. Whitaker went into the house and returned with a block of matches and with a calmness not altogether pretense she handed it to the commanding officer and said, 'Sir, I want to look into the eyes of a man who can stoop so low as to burn the home of a helpless woman and her children.' Up to this time the drastic methods, later adopted by Sherman in Georgia, had not been resorted to by Union men. The soldiers turned away and the house was saved."[26]*

CHAPTER 3

FROM THE GROUND UP

What eventually became the town of Sarasota remained primarily wilderness throughout most of the nineteenth century. In 1883 there were only 6 households north of Whitaker Bayou, 26 in "Sara Sota", 12 at Bee Ridge, 3 at Fruitville, 13 at Miakka, 15 at Osprey, and 2 at Venice-Nokomis. This was soon to change.[1]

On distant shores a British corporation operating out of Edinburgh, Scotland saw the opportunity to turn sand into gold. The company, the Florida Mortgage and Investment Co., Ltd. purchased 50,000 acres of Sarasota for $1 per acre. Sir John Gillespie, who served as the Archbishop of Canterbury, and other shareholders decided to build a town to lure settlers to the new world. They platted the land for the first time, designing a town. With Great Britain suffering an economic recession, dozens of Scots were eager to invest the price of 100 pounds sterling for a 40 acre estate and an opportunity for a better life in the "small but modern town of Sarasota."[2,3]

Upon their arrival in 1885, the Scots discovered that Sarasota was not yet the "paradise on Earth" that they had been promised. Sixty-eight faces crowded the rails of the steamer and gazed at the white sandy beaches. The beaches were indeed beautiful, but where were the hotels, businesses, shops, and streets that they were told of? Enthusiasm turned to discontent when they learned that the town of Sarasota was little more than the white sandy beaches and the wilderness beyond. Anything else existed only in concept on the Town Platt and in the promises from the company's local manager, Mr. Tate. If not for the hospitality of the local crackers, they may not have survived. Three months after leaving Scotland, all but a few headed back.[4,5,6,7]

Although the majority of the Scots departed, the Florida Mortgage Company was still resolute in their desire to build the village of Sarasota. The company

The original platt of the town of Sarasota as filed in 1886 in Manatee County.

seemed to have both the finances and the resolve to make its dreams into realities. Mr. A.C. Acton arrived in town and served as the company's local manager, replacing Mr. Tate who abruptly left town when he heard that some of the hot-headed settlers were planning to come calling with shotguns in hand. The company instructed Acton to begin building the town "at once," and Sarasota's first building boom began.[8,9,10]

Sarasota lacked many of the necessities that a town needs in its infancy to entice potential residents. No lodging facilities existed for visitors, workers, or prospective residents. A wharf was needed where vessels could dock to deliver the materials that would be required to build the town from the ground up. Saltwater surrounded the settlers, but fresh water for drinking remained scarce. Finally, the streets stretched out as little more than paths worn from the infrequent foot traffic. Much needed to be done.

At first when Acton started hiring workers, there were too few to accomplish the tasks needed by the fledgling town. But soon, workmen from elsewhere were lured by the prospect of employment. The sudden influx of masons, carpenters, and others left the town with a dilemma of where to accommodate the workers, who occupied every available space. Workers camped on the beach, rented sleeping space in the many schooners anchored in Sarasota Bay, and constructed little wood shanties to serve as temporary housing. Regardless of where they slept, they considered themselves fortunate to have found employment.[11,12,13]

One of the first orders of business was the construction of a wharf to open the town to the many trading vessels that sailed the waters. Without imports and exports the town would surely falter. The pier, soon to be the gateway to a bustling downtown, would extend directly into Sarasota Bay from the foot of Main Street. Work on the pier commenced early in January of 1886, and for three months settlers and workmen toiled chest deep in the bitter cold water for their wages of two dollars per day. A rare snowfall a few days before work on the pier began did not stifle the enthusiasm. Because of the lack of machinery piles of pine were set by hand until the deck of heavy lumber was finally laid. A fifty foot square extension was built at the far end upon which workers erected a warehouse. The pier's usefulness became immediately evident as schooners, steamboats and other vessels soon began delivering goods and travelers to Sarasota.[14,15]

While the construction of the pier was still underway, Main Street was in the process of being cleared and prepared for development. Ditches were dug on the side of the street for drainage with the extra dirt placed in the center of the road to form a crown. The sides of Main Street were lined with a wooden sidewalk, which gave Main street an air of sophistication

The Higel Dock at the foot of Main Street was purchased by Harry L. Higel from the Florida Mortgage and Investment Company. Dave Broadway operated his oyster pavillion from the building on the right.

Early buildings featured wood walls and shingles and they were constructed dangerously close to one another. Shown is the Clark and Calhoun Store and J.C. Calhoun Residence on Main Street in 1903.

and served to tie the business district together. Main Street was initially cleared from the wharf to Five Points but soon the remainder of the downtown streets would also be defined.[16,17]

Concurrently with the construction of the pier, activity was bustling at the opposite end of Main Street, at Five Points. Construction of the Sarasota House began in 1886. Its placement at the northeast corner of Main Street and Central Avenue provided a superb view of Sarasota Bay and afforded the virgin lots along Main Street the potential for development. The Sarasota House, complete with a dining room and twenty beds, was to be a place of lodging for those of moderate means, including many workman who arrived with the first building boom.[18]

As the town began to grow, greater and more reliable supplies of fresh water were needed. The city contracted to drill an artisan well at Five Points. Many structures such as the Sarasota House and the Desoto Hotel built in 1887 drew their supply of fresh water from this early water source. The artisan well had its limitations. It adequately served the domestic water needs but could not supply sufficient quantities of water to use for fire protection.[19,20]

Sanitary sewers were still handled the old-fashioned way. Each household had an outdoor privy, for which the owner was responsible. Hotels such as the Desoto Hotel drained directly into Sarasota Bay.

By the late 1880's the village of Sarasota began to resemble the platt originally proposed by the Florida Mortgage and Investment Company. Buildings seemed to spring up on Main Street like clover. The wooden structures speckled the street at first, then filled every available lot. Sarasotans now had the entreprenual spirit, and everyone wanted his shop located in the heart of the business district. As a result businesses got progressively closer together until the wood walls of adjacent businesses actually touched.

Dr. Thomas Wallace serves as an example of the determination possessed by the remaining settlers. He was one of the original Scot settlers who had sufficient perseverance to remain through the hardships. He erected a one and a half story house on the north side of Main Street about one hundred feet from Palm Avenue. He established a one-cot clinic by dedicating a room of his home for the treatment of patients. Wallace was also the first physician to prepare and dispense medications, which he did from a room adjacent to the clinic.[21,22,23]

William Whitaker's sons, Furman and Will constructed a general store on the south side of Main Street almost directly opposite Wallace's home and clinic. Prior to the arrival of the Scottish settlers, one store existed in town. The company store, operated by the Florida Investment Corporation, was small and carried only the bare essentials. Lacking competition, it had little incentive to offer a fair price to the settlers. The new Whitaker store touted shelves full of merchandise and stocked everything from tobacco plugs to gunpowder. Sarasotans saw this as a sure sign of progress.[24,25]

Hamlin Whitaker was also an enterprising young man who constructed a meat market at Main Street and Palm Avenue. He and a partner built and operated a livery stable at Main Street and Palm Avenue on the site of the future Sarasota Hotel, currently known as the Palm Towers Building. Stables with their wood construction and flammable content of hay would later cause several destructive fires.

in building a hotel that was certainly one of the finest on the West Coast of Florida.[26,27]

Sarasotans enjoyed their first building boom during the late 1880's and felt they were constructing a road to riches. They did not yet realize that in years to come they would pay a heavy price for their buildings' construction techniques. The same factors that allowed structures to be rapidly and profitably built also predisposed them to suffer tremendous losses to fire.

The common denominator to every building constructed during Sarasota's first boom was wood. The materials, combined with construction techniques and a lack of awareness, caused the town to learn some

Main Street looking from the top of the Belle Haven Inn at the foot of Main Street towards Five Points.

By the late 1880's Sarasota still lacked a hotel for people of "wealth and influence." The Florida Mortgage and Investment Company saw the opportunity and built the Desoto Hotel to cater to wealthy tourists and potential settlers. The hotel consisted of three stories with a widows' watch above the third floor. Built on Sarasota Bay at Main Street and Gulfstream Avenue, its view of the bay was unmatched. Many tourists returned year after year to gaze upon Sarasota Bay and perhaps daydream about the day's catch of tarpon. The Florida Mortgage and Investment Company succeeded

painful and expensive lessons. Although these lessons had already been learned by other growing cities like San Francisco and Chicago, Sarasotans would soon experience them firsthand.

Cut lumber was shipped in from Cedar Key, Apalachicola, and Pensacola. Its ready availability and economical price made it the ideal building material for a town that had not yet established a productive economy. The frame, walls, floor, and roof of most Sarasota buildings were pine, which quickly dried when exposed to the hot Florida sun. After a few years,

The Bay View House featured large comfortable rooms and baths for two dollars per day. Its view of Sarasota Bay was magnificent. Wood was the most common construction material of the time because it was readily available and less expensive than masonry. The sign reads "Bay View House."

COURTESY SARASOTA COUNTY DEPARTMENT OF HISTORICAL RESOURCES

therefore, the building became tinder dry.[28]

Generally the chimney and foundation were the only features of the early buildings that were not made of wood. The foundation was created by a mason who cemented brick in a stack to create footers set around the perimeter of the building and at several points in its center. These footers bore the full weight of the structure. Upon the footers rested the floor joists, heavy lumber upon which the wood floor would be laid. The footers provided a firm foundation upon which the entire stability of the building would depend. They also served to keep the structure elevated to protect it from flooding caused by heavy seasonal rain. What proved a blessing during the rainy season proved a curse during a fire. By locating the floor several feet above the ground, the builders subjected the wooden underside of the structure to the flames and radiant heat given off when nearby structures caught fire.

Most buildings of the day were constructed using a balloon-style construction. Balloon construction inherently created voids within the walls and floors of the structure. Thus, when a fire occurred, it rapidly traveled throughout the walls, setting the entire structure ablaze within minutes.

Wood-shake shingles, created by splitting pieces of wood along the grain, also created a fire hazard. When nailed to the roof in overlapping layers, they formed a beautiful and effective barrier to the elements. Wood shingles caused the same problems that they had caused for earlier settlers: their rough surfaces caught flying embers that went aloft during a fire, thus providing a ready source of ignition for other buildings. By rapidly spreading the fire to even distant buildings the combination of flying embers and wood-shake shingles threatened the entire town.

Those hearty individuals willing to devote their effort to build the town were a special breed. Life in the 1880's was hard, and many of the luxuries of a modern society were simply not yet available in Sarasota. The town primarily functioned between sunrise and sunset. Work was grueling and began at or before sunrise. Candles and lamps provided the necessary light at night for domestic uses because the town had not yet made arrangements for the new innovation of electrical lighting. The open flame of candles and lamps created a great hazard; they would later be responsible for several devastating fires.

CHAPTER 4

BUILT TO BURN

The individuals who forged Sarasota out of the wilderness were an independent group who desired to create for themselves a better life. Not surprisingly they desired greater autonomy in government in order to direct their own destiny. By an act of the Florida legislature and governor on April 30, 1903, Sarasota became a legally incorporated town.[1]

The town fathers realized that this young town depended on further development and a continued influx of tourists and new residents to assure its future. The town ordinances, therefore, were written with a conscious effort to keep Sarasota the most desirable place on the Gulf Coast. Issues such as chastity, vagrancy, gambling, animal cruelty, and privy maintenance were regulated by ordinance. Although Sarasota had not yet experienced any serious fires except for those caused by the Seminoles and Union soldiers, the town fathers were already aware of the potential for fire. The ordinances dealing with fire addressed three areas of concern: hazardous acts, construction, and storage.[2]

Hazardous acts by individuals were the most likely

Once started fire rapidly consumed Sarasota's wooden structures. Without a fire department citizens could do little but watch and pray.

to cause a serious fire and were addressed first. The ordinance read in part that: "If any person shall go, or send a servant, with an open or uncovered light of any kind, into any stable or barn,... such person shall be fined in a sum not exceeding $50 or be imprisoned in the common jail or calaboose, not more than 20 days." The penalty was appropriate when one considers that a single violation could potentially burn down the entire town. The ordinance proved effective until February 9, 1910, when the Bradley Livery Stables were destroyed by fire. The Bradley Stables were the first of many stables to be lost by fire.[3,4]

The town calaboose served as a deterrent to crime in Sarasota. The small and simple wood structure became quite unpleasant during Sarasota's hot summers, although it was not very secure. The local deputy sheriff of Manatee County, of which Sarasota was a part, was J.W. Harvey. He was occasionally called upon to arrest a roustabout who drank too much and became disorderly. Harvey told of several occasions when he placed his prisoner in the wooden jail and closed the door, but by the time he walked around to the back of the jail, the prisoner had already kicked the boards off the rear wall and was crawling out.[5,6]

Town Calaboose in 1911. The hot Florida sun made the lockup an uncomfortable place to spend the days. It served as a deterrent to crime.

The second ordinance to deal with hazardous acts stated that persons were prohibited from burning trash or refuse material within the corporate limits of the town, after sunset, or within sixty feet of any structure without written permission from the mayor. Violators also received a $50 fine and 20 days in the calaboose.[7]

The throwing of fireworks such as fire balls, fire crackers, and rockets, within the town was considered too dangerous to allow routinely. Reserved for special occasions, they were permitted only with written permission from the mayor for special occasions such as Christmas and New Years, but were restricted from an area of the town designated as the fire limits. Likewise the discharge of any firearm within the town limits was deemed unsafe and was covered by the same section of the ordinance. Gunfire, however, would become a familiar sound which repeatedly awakened the sleeping town of Sarasota and served as a community fire alarm.[8,9,10]

Town ordinances did not address construction materials and techniques with the exception of chimneys. Homeowners fortunate enough to afford a stove to cook inside their home were required to have a stone pipe or brick flue rising above the ceiling. Cooking inside was considered more dangerous than cooking in detached kitchens, which was still prevalent in the houses of the less affluent. Other aspects of construction would not be controlled by ordinance for some time.[11]

Storage was the third concern to those who drafted the town's first ordinances since many common household items were considered dangerous when stored in large quantities. For example, gunpowder was a necessity for the still isolated town and could be found in most homes and in larger quantities in many businesses. Furthermore every home and business depended on candles or kerosine lamps for illumination after sunset, so quantities of kerosene oil were also on hand for daily use. In an effort to limit the hazards associated with the storage of combustible or explosive products, the town fathers required that businesses and houses store gunpowder in tin cases and only in quantities of three kegs or less. Also, merchants could not draw, weigh, or in any manner expose for sale any gunpowder, kerosene oil, turpentine, or other combustible or explosive liquid after early candle light — sunset.[12]

Lacking a fire department, the town marshall was charged with inspecting chimneys, lamps, and lights of all kinds of material, and the storage of gunpowder and inflammable materials. His diverse duties also required him to inspect privies semi-monthly, arrest vagrants

Early Sarasotans gather for a weekend picnic, with an abundance of wild game providing plenty of food for all.

COURTESY LUCILLE HAYES EVERETT

and gamblers, and otherwise maintain law and order.[13]

As the years passed, the impending threat of fire hovered over Sarasota like a dark cloud. Nearly every building was composed of wood, housed flammable or explosive elements, and was adjacent to other buildings with the same characteristics. To make matters worse the use of fire to cook or light a room or path was commonplace. The town fathers realized that they had created a formula for disaster and decided to resolve the problem by using a proactive approach.

The Fire Limit Ordinance, signed into law September 8, 1909, established a geographical area of the town known as the "fire limits" and regulated the construction, alteration, repairing, and rebuilding of structures within the fire limits. In its main section the ordinance forbade the continued use of wood and other flammable materials on the outside of any structure erected within the fire limits.[14,15]

Under the Fire Limit Ordinance, existing buildings could not be altered, repaired, or rebuilt when the total expenses exceeded $200 unless the work was done using non-combustible materials. All new buildings were to be constructed of stone, brick, cement, corrugated iron, or other "fire-proof" material. Plans and specifications, along with a five dollar fee to cover the cost of inspection, were required by the office of the town clerk prior to the commencement of construction in order to receive a permit. Violators of the Fire Limit Ordinance received up to $100 in fines and 30 days in the calaboose. In future years the fire limits would expand as the town grew in size, and its requirements became more stringent. The Fire Limit Ordinance, however, did not remove the dangerous conditions that already existed within the town.[16]

First "Fireproof" building. Located at Five Points, the Bank of Sarasota was built in 1905. The town's first library in 1907 was located on the second floor. The watering trough in the foreground was originally used for horses and cattle.

SARASOTA COUNTY
DEPARTMENT OF
HISTORICAL RESOURCES

CHAPTER 5

BUCKETS AND BRAWN

"Again the cry of FIRE startled the town of Sarasota, and the citizens turned out en masse. The Bay View House was fully ablaze when the fire was discovered." These words screamed across the pages of the *Sarasota Times* and told the story of the February 8, 1910 event that would have a lasting effect on the town.[1]

The Bay View House was located on the northwest corner of Main Street and Palm Avenue. Its construction was typical of the day, built of yellow pine using wood frame construction. When the afternoon fire was first discovered, smoke already billowed from the upper part of the building as the fire gained rapid headway. Without a fire department, the residents could not save the structure, which was already extensively consumed with fire and in danger of collapse.[2,3]

Every able-bodied citizen, however, was on hand to lend assistance because in a town as small as Sarasota, they were all neighbors. Those that were too young or unable to help watched in awe. The fire appeared to start just under the roof, which provided enough time for willing hands to remove the furniture.[4]

Henry Behrens, who had arrived in town just two days before, organized the firefighting efforts. Behrens had no problem gaining cooperation because he was the only one in town with any formal experience in firefighting. Having served as a volunteer firefighter in Cincinnati, Ohio, his experience proved invaluable.[5,6]

During the Bay View House fire the radiant heat was so intense that many people thought it impossible to save the Burton Block, which was located across the street and just over eighty feet away. Many of the town's men proved themselves to be heros as they climbed onto the roof of the Burton Block buildings. Meanwhile, bucket brigades formed and passed water up to the men on the rooftops. While breathing acrid choking smoke, the men desperately fought to save the structures by keeping the roof and exposed sides of the building wet.[7]

The town's fears of a conflagration seemed well founded as the fire continued to spread beyond the Bay View House. An old storage building owned by Harry L. Higel stood to the west of the Bay View House. The building was used to store lumber for Mr. Higel's proposed new structure. The lumber, which was already cut and ready for erection, was soon ablaze as was the building, with only a small portion of the wood salvaged from the building before the fire became too intense.[8]

The northwesterly winds showered sparks and ashes onto structures blocks away. The wood shingles on the roofs rapidly ignited, endangering the dwellings of Mrs. Bass, Mrs. Boyett and Mr. Knight. Fortunately, the fires were immediately discovered and extinguished. Out houses belonging to Mr. Wilson, the editor of the *Sarasota Times*, caught fire. Mr. and Mrs. Josh Walker, who were passing by, took charge and put out the fires. Grass lots blocks away also burned, thereby threatening to spread the fire still farther.[9]

Later that day, the town expected the fire to gain still greater proportions. The Wallace House was evacuated, and the people in the *Sarasota Times* office prepared to

The Bay View House was located at the northwest corner of Main Street and Palm Avenue. It burned on February 8, 1910. It is often confused with the Bay View Hotel, which was located on Mango Avenue and burned in 1912.

move on short notice. These buildings would surely be destroyed if the Burton block caught fire.[10]

As the men on the roof of the Burton Block continued their desperate fight, they suffered injury. Several of them were blistered and burned, and all were physically exhausted. Mr. Sines suffered from the intense heat and was forced to take refuge behind the chimney.[11]

The battle continued until the Bay View House collapsed and the intensity of the fire gradually dissipated. The entire town breathed a sigh of relief and began to examine the losses. The Bay View House was insured, but Harry Higel lacked insurance on his lumber.[12]

The town had gained a reverent respect for fire. They now realized its awesome destructive ability. They also knew that they must discover a better way to control the fire menace.

The town was still recuperating from the arduous battle of the previous day. Discussion of how the entire town was nearly consumed by fire dominated every conversation as stories of great danger and courageous firefighting efforts abounded. Residents put out their lanterns for the evening and retired for a restful nights sleep, one that would soon be disturbed. Their slumber was abruptly interrupted by the clanging of the town bell and the familiar cries of FIRE!

Between ten and eleven o'clock the fire was discovered. The fire's location was unmistakable, and folks raced towards it like moths attracted to a candle. The fire had started on the second floor of a large three story building owned by A.W. Bradley, which housed a stable on the ground floor, the Bradley Board and Lodging House on the second floor, and the Camp of the Woodmen of the World on the third floor.[13]

Similar to the Bay View House fire, the Bradley Livery Stables fire grew rapidly and extended beyond the building in which it had originated. It also consumed the dwelling of A. W. Bradley and McGinty's lumber yard located in the rear. Several freight cars of the Seaboard Airline Railroad were severely damaged, and the important depot and freight house seemed endangered. The feed and lumber store of Jones and McAlpin appeared to be the next to burn. Had its walls and roof not been constructed of metal, it would have joined the fate of the others. The Fire Limit Ordinance had finally proven justified.[14]

With memories of the preceding days events in mind, all hands worked to fill buckets and empty them onto the fire and on the sides and roofs of neighboring businesses and dwellings. Others assisted in trying to salvage furniture and personal belongings ahead of the ravaging flames.[15]

The *Sarasota Times* credited the town's folks with "super human efforts" in saving E. B. Grantham's dwelling, C. C. McGinty's office and dwelling, and E. W. Redd's building. Without their efforts, the fire certainly could have swept through the town unrestrained. In two days of hard work, most of the town of Sarasota was saved by buckets and brawn.[16]

City Livery Stables located at the northeast corner of Main Street and Lemon Avenue. The stable, owned and operated by A.W. Bradley and Sons, was destroyed by fire on February 9, 1910. The dwelling of A.W. Bradley, which was constructed just left of the stable, was also destroyed. The dwelling of Eliza Grantham (right) was saved.

CHAPTER 6

WALK BEFORE YOU RUN

Much of Sarasota laid in ashes from the Bay View House and Bradley Livery Stable fires. The ruins made it apparent that if the town was going to survive, it would need an organized fire department.

Henry Behrens, who had assumed a leadership role in organizing the firefighting efforts of the two previous days, compiled a small group of volunteers who were able to assist should the threat of fire again resurface. The high-spirited group was bound together by their common desire to save the town from destruction by fire. They were sometimes referred to as fire laddies, a name which reflects their Scottish ancestry. They proceeded with enthusiasm and good intentions but lacked the proper equipment to fight fire.

Nearly eight months later, the town council took steps to protect the town by voting to appoint J. L.

J.W. Harvey's blacksmith shop located on Main Street between Lemon and Orange Avenues. J.W. Harvey built Sarasota's first hook and ladder truck in 1911. Firemen relied on their brawn and determination to pull it by hand through the sandy streets. Left: R.S.(Bob) Franklin, son of G.W. Franklin, one time mayor of Sarasota. Right: Alice Titus Franklin.

Truck No. 1, Sarasota Volunteer Fire Company's first ladder truck.

Houle as a "fire inspector of buildings" on October 4, 1910. He began to perform regular inspections of existing buildings and careful examinations of newly constructed ones.[1]

In a dramatic step by the town council, on October 11, 1910, a citizens committee was appointed to investigate the acquisition of a chemical engine and hook and ladder truck for the town. Appointed to the committee were J. L. Houle as chairman, Mr. and Mrs. William Jeffcot, and G. L. Roberts. The counsel also received, "a verbal proposition from the Eureka Fire Hose Company regarding fire hose and other firefighting equipment." The council voted to bond $20,000 for the installation of a water and sewer system, which included fire hydrants.[2]

The fire committee raised almost all the funds to purchase the chemical engine and hook and ladder truck through private subscriptions, but fund raising efforts fell short by $125. The town council generously agreed to provide the balance. At the beginning of 1911, the town turned out to marvel over their new equipment.[3,4]

The Eureka double chemical engine was a beauty with its polished black metal tank which glistened in the sunlight. The tank contained water in which bicarbonate of soda was dissolved. When sulfuric acid was added to the mixture, carbon dioxide gas formed. Enough pressure would then build up in the closed container to expel the water under great pressure. The speed of the reaction meant that the town's new chemical engine was ready for action on a moments notice. Unfortunately, the engine could be readied more rapidly than it could be moved. Volunteers had to pull the heavy chemical engine through the town's sandy streets by hand. It was hard work that exhausted the volunteers even before they started fighting the fire.

The town's first hook and ladder truck was built in the local blacksmith shop of J.W. Harvey. Like the chemical engine, it was pulled by hand through the town's streets. Its cargo of sturdy wooden ladders were

Sarasota purchased three hand-pulled hose reels called jumpers in 1911, the same year that the municipal hydrant system was installed. The jumpers carried hose, which was connected to the hydrant nearest a fire and unwound from the reel as it was pulled to the fire. By 1915, Sarasota owned hose from four different manufacturers: Paragon, Eureka, Red Cross, and Boston.

heavy and added to the burden. The truck also carried hooks for pulling down the walls of burning buildings to stop the spread of the fire. A lantern served for illuminating the route to a fire and for sending semaphore signals at night.

Local entrepreneurs were pleased that the new equipment reduced their fire insurance rates by approximately five percent. But the majority of citizens did not have fire insurance on their dwellings; it was a luxury that most simply could not afford. Prior to the arrival of the firefighting equipment, when a building fire did occur, generally the entire structure was destroyed. Helpless families only watched as their homes and precious belongings turned to ashes. Neighbors and families did what they could by providing a temporary place to sleep, clothes, and food until other arrangements could be made.[5]

The chairman of the fire committee, J. Louis Houle, advertised a meeting for the "organization of the Sarasota Fire Department" to be held the evening of March 20, 1911. "All men who are interested in the welfare of the town" were requested to attend. The meeting was an attempt to formally organize the group of volunteers into a chemical company and a separate hook and ladder company.[6,7]

The town's new chemical engine made its debut performance on the afternoon of April 12, 1911. A small trash fire in the rear of the city market was fanned by the wind and spread to a sizable pile of rubbish. From there the fire spread rapidly, igniting the underside of Dr. Joseph Halton's office. The new fire engine was pulled through the town streets until it and the volunteers arrived on scene. Working in conjunction with a bucket brigade, the volunteer squad not only saved Dr. Halton's office but also the McNight Boarding House and another business. The volunteers demonstrated their ability to confine the fire to the building of origin by preventing its further spread.[8]

Simultaneously, with the installation of a deep well, water works, water mains, and fire hydrants in 1911, the town authorized the purchase of three hand drawn hose carts and other additional fire equipment amounting to $1120 from the Eureka Fire Hose Manufacturing company. Each of the hose carts, called hose jumpers, carried several hundred feet of woven fire hose wrapped on a reel. The fire department now consisted of a handful of volunteers, a hook and ladder truck, a chemical engine, and three hose jumpers. Sarasota now had the humble beginnings of a fire department but still lacked both a formal organization and official recognition as a practicing fire department from the town.[9]

CHAPTER 7

A HUMBLE BEGINNING

The citizens of Sarasota in 1911 had just invested in firefighting equipment to secure the safety of the town. They naturally felt somewhat insecure turning it over to a group of volunteer firemen who lacked organization and formal training. The solution seemed obvious to the town council.

The town council approved an ordinance to "create and regulate a fire department in the town of Sarasota." Ordinance number 55, which was drafted and signed into law by Mayor H.S. Smith on September 26, 1911, formally organized the Sarasota Fire Department. Members of the loosely constructed group felt they had taken a great stride forward by gaining the official recognition of the town.[1]

The ordinance established how the newly created department was to fit into the civic life of the community. It instructed the town council to designate a fire committee and gave it responsibility over the fire department. A fire chief was to be appointed by the mayor with input from the town council. The fire chief was answerable to the fire committee and ultimately the town council. This pecking order was carefully set up by the town council to avoid relinquishing too much control to the fire department.[2]

The fire chief's first task was to submit the names of ten active members of the fire department to the clerk of the circuit court for the purpose of exempting them from jury duty. The newly acquired fire equipment made obtaining volunteers an easy task, but choosing only ten was difficult. The volunteers saw themselves as gallant heros who did nothing less than save the town from destruction by fire. The importance of the volunteers was reinforced by the granting of the right of way over the streets and alleys to the fire department while it went to or returned from a fire. Any person convicted of interfering with the lawful duties of the fire department faced a ten dollar fine and/or ten days imprisonment. The same applied for anyone who maliciously gave a false alarm.[3]

The fire chief was charged with the overall responsibility for the functioning of the department. He was responsible for seeing that the equipment was well cared for and ready for immediate use. He maintained records of all alarms and actual fires. Most of all, he maintained a sense of discipline both on the fire ground and during routine functions. Disobedience was not tolerated. Any violation of the rules of the fire department or disobedience of any order from a superior officer while on duty resulted in dismissal. Offenders were also fined ten dollars and imprisoned for ten days.[4]

With the ordinance established, Sarasota needed to appoint a chief. Sarasota's newly elected mayor, Harry L. Higel, wrote a letter on this point in 1911 to many of the local business leaders saying:

"Dear Sir:

You are paying too much fire insurance; Sarasota can be made rated a third class town instead of a fourth class if we get our fire department regulated and established properly. I wish to appoint a fire chief. It is to your

Taking a rest from the growing pains of building a town. Men and women segregated to socialize while awaiting a parade in 1912. Looking north on lower Main Street from the pier towards Five Points. To the right is the Belle Haven Inn, formerly the Desoto Hotel, constructed in 1887. The Orange Blossom Club Apartments currently stand on the site.

interest personally, so I suggest that you meet me at the council chamber on January 4th at 7:30 p.m. to see what we can do for the best interest of the town."[5]

The council held the meeting as scheduled and appointed Henry Behrens as the first official chief of the Sarasota Volunteer Fire Company. Prior to that time, the department did not have an official fire chief.

Although Behrens had organized the department after the Bay View House fire, J.M. Schneider was elected by the members to serve as the volunteer fire chief. Schneider, however, was not officially recognized by the town council and was replaced by Behrens a few months later. With the appointment of Chief Behrens, the Sarasota Volunteer Fire Company was renamed the Sarasota Fire Department.[6,7,8]

HENRY BEHRENS

Whether it was coincidence or fate that brought Henry Behrens to Sarasota just two days before the infamous Bay View House fire may never be known. It is certain that his arrival was a blessing for the fire department. Behrens provided the strength and leadership that was desperately needed during a vulnerable time in its development.

Henry George Behrens was of German ancestry. His father, Henry Behrens, Senior, moved to Cincinnati, Ohio from Hanover, Germany. Henry Senior began as a carpenter's apprentice and soon became a very successful contractor. He married Margaret Ortman, and together they raised six children, one of whom would eventually become Sarasota's first fire chief.[1]

Born on November 16, 1883, Henry George Behrens grew up in Cincinnati. His zest for life was unquenchable, and every day presented an opportunity for a new experience. Behrens packed a lifetime of living into every day. As a young man he worked for a time as a carpenter's apprentice becoming a fine craftsman and learning the art of cabinetry. John Ringling hired Behrens in 1914 to do cabinet work in his yacht. He also crafted furniture and staircases for Sarasota's prestigious homes such as those of the Palmers, Caples, and Ringlings.[2,3,4]

Carpentry fell by the wayside when Behrens apprenticed himself to a gunsmith. Talent and determination made learning easy. In fact, at age fourteen he made his first gun, a single-shot, breech-loading percussion Derringer. Henry not only learned the job but furthered the art. During his lifetime he created hundreds of guns, many of which were original unpatented designs. He contended that he built guns for himself, and therefore there was no reason for him to patent his ideas. Many of his designs were later mass produced by others. Henry was once asked, "Why did you never try gun manufacturing?" Behrens answered as expected. "I never wanted to. I had all the guns I wanted right here." Behren's guns were remarkable because they were all made with hand tools, not with machines. Each piece was hand crafted with a precision that would rival today's industry. In addition, Behren's shooting matched his workmanship. According to a *Sarasota Times* newspaper article, "He once killed 16 quail and a rabbit with one shot from a borrowed Winchester shotgun."[5,6]

While in Cincinnati Behrens served as a volunteer fireman. During this time he gained the knowledge and experience that would later prove invaluable to Sarasota. In Cincinnati the seed was planted and Behrens's love of firefighting grew. He would not have any further exposure to firefighting until his arrival to Sarasota.[7]

After leaving Cincinnati, he traveled west for a spell and lived the life of a cowboy. The difficult work of driving cattle fit his personality. At 27 years of age, Behrens found himself in Sarasota. After only two days in town, he responded to and took charge at the great Bay View House fire. His display of leadership earned him the position of fire chief.[8]

Early fire chiefs were typically individuals with a physical stature big enough to convince firemen to

Handsome Henry and Wild Bill. Henry Behrens (right) poses in front of post office boxes at Sarasota's new post office. Constructed in 1934 at the northeast corner of Orange Avenue and Ringling Boulevard, it is now known as the Federal Building.

obey their commands, by force if necessary. Behrens was no exception. He stood tall, with broad shoulders, and was straightforward when he was running the department. His presence commanded attention, and his men respected him enough to never put him to the test. While fighting fires his voice could be heard booming above the commotion, giving direction and encouragement.

Behrens was an active and well respected member of the community. While serving as fire chief, he also

If his stature didn't command respect, his gun did. Behrens helped keep law and order as a deputy marshall for Manatee County from 1911 to 1921. He concurrently served in Sarasota as fire chief.

helped to maintain law and order. From 1911 to 1921, he served as a deputy marshall of Manatee County, when Sarasota was still part of Manatee. He served as Sarasota's first night chief of police from 1928 until 1932. Behrens was an excellent marksman but preferred to maintain order with a nightstick. Behrens faithfully raised the Stars and Stripes every morning in honor of Sarasota's servicemen at the Five Points flagpole, which was erected in 1917. Behrens also served during World War I on the Ringling yacht as a member of the harbor patrol. During the war, the luxury yacht was equipped with two guns and pressed into service to protect the town from enemy threats that might come by water.[9,10,11]

Behrens had another side that was visible when not working; he was certainly noticed by the ladies of the town who considered him to be handsome and a

Henry Behrens served as an officer in the U.S. Naval Reserves during WW I as a member of the harbor patrol.

gentleman. Even little girls swooned over him. His sense of humor kept even the most stone-faced individual in stitches, and people always counted on him for a good story.[12]

Henry's love life, however, was bitter sweet. He was lucky enough to have loved, but not all his marriages had happy endings. He first married Annie Bear of Venice in 1910. His second marriage to Anna

The *"Echo II" owned by Henry Behrens won the speedboat race at the annual Fourth of July Celebration in 1912. Foot races, sack races, motorcycle races, greased pole climbing, greased pig catching, and a pie eating contest added to the festivities.*

Stephens in 1916 ended with the tragic illness and death of his beloved wife only one and a half years later. Behrens proposal to Louise Keller, whom he had known for many years, arrived at her Cincinnati home in the form of a postcard. The correspondence read, "Say, don't I look lonesome? See that empty seat. It

needs someone to fill it. Will you do it? — Henry." Miss Keller's enthusiastic yes was the culmination of their long-time romance. After her arrival by train, they were immediately married by Justice of the Peace C. O. Teate in 1918. They remained united in wedded bliss until her death in 1956.[13,14,15,16]

Although he had many talents and held many positions of employment, Behrens loved gunsmithing with all his heart. His death certificate dated December 14, 1967 listed his employment as he wanted to be remembered, Gunsmith.[17]

This modest sign in front of the Behrens' residence is to the point. He was known as the "best gunsmith for miles around."

Henry Behrens proposed to his future wife on this 1918 post card. Behrens is seated in a Model White Chief's Car in front of the Desoto Hotel. After he drove this manufacturer's demo, the department placed their order and received delivery in 1920.

COURTESY JOSEPHINE WENSEL

CHAPTER 9

THE FIRST FIREHOUSE

The town received its first fire equipment early in 1911 but for several months had no provisions to house it. On August 2, 1911 the town council appointed a committee composed of Mr. Halton, Mr. Burns, and Mr. Seale, to find an appropriate location to erect a fire station. By January 9, 1912 the committee's work was done, and the town council sat in special session to select the final location and to plan for the upcoming construction. The triangle-shaped property located at Pineapple and Lemon Avenues was chosen. The construction was completed post-haste and by March of 1912 the Sarasota Fire Department was the proud owner of their first fire station. Its new address was 125 South Pineapple Avenue. The stone building beside the station was the new town jail, and in back of the station on Lemon Avenue stood the town water works and ice plant.[1,2,3]

The fire department proudly paraded their equipment down Pineapple Avenue and to their new home. The town cheered enthusiastically in support. Fourteen men lined up with their equipment in front of the new station for a photograph.[4]

The interior walls and rafters of the station were constructed of wood but the outside walls and roof were of corrugated metal. The fire department did not want to risk embarrassment should a flying ember

Sarasota's first fire station constructed in 1912. It was located at Pineapple and Lemon Avenues. Left to right: J.K. Hill, Hollis Bacon, Ben Hill, Frank Roberts, Cy Byrd, Ben Seale, Myron Spencer, Henry Behrens (fire chief), Irvin Riorseth, Valley Hill, Rube Hayes, Leonard Rudd, Bill Adams, and George Willis.

ignite the walls or roof and burn the fire station down. The floor was of wood, and the front and rear of the structure both had two doors large enough to allow the equipment to be pulled through. One wall was lined with enough hooks to hang the helmets and slickers of the volunteers.

attempted to rescue a burning freight car by moving it off the dock. Since its cargo of lumber continued to burn and threaten a number of residences, the order was given to push it back onto the dock to protect the remainder of the town. Wind drove the black volumes of smoke and burning embers over the Belle

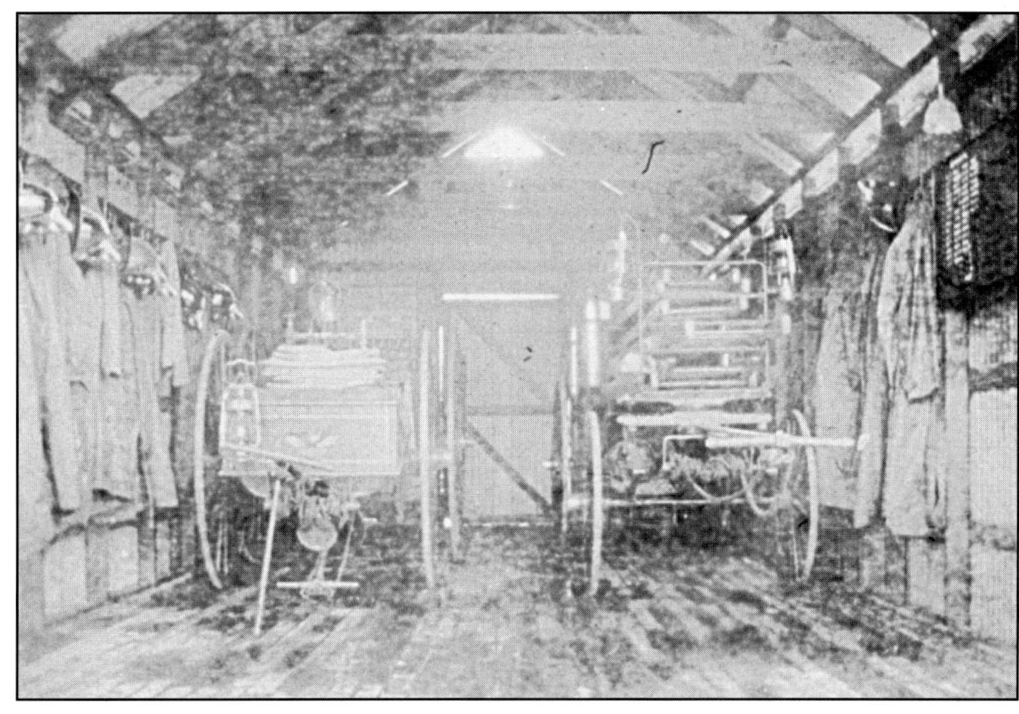

Interior view of Sarasota's first owned fire station. It was constructed in 1912 to house Sarasota's hand-drawn chemical engine (left) and hand drawn ladder truck (right).

The following year the department built a wood structure in the rear of the station which looked like a toboggan run. The large slope provided a surface for the draining and drying of fire hose. The structure would gain frequent use after the many fires that would occur during the next several years.[5]

The first serious fire of 1912 occurred on February 26 at approximately ten p.m.. The railroad dock and fish houses owned by the Sarasota Fish and Oyster Company burned brightly against the night sky. Sarasotans by the hundreds crowded the shoreline to witness the blaze. The fire grew steadily as it consumed the dock and structures. Stores of gasoline and oil intensified the fire. Fishing vessels were cut free, and nets were dropped from the pier onto the drifting vessels in hopes of limiting the losses. But one of the vessels was already ablaze along with a great deal of fishing tackle and nets. Many of the townsmen

Haven Inn. The anxious guests were relieved, however, when a change in wind direction removed them from harm's way.[6]

The fire started in the little engine room occupied by Mr. Vivian, a machinist for the company. Two fishermen reportedly heard cries for help from this room. Noticing a light in the upper part of the building, they hastened to assist. They tried both doors only to find them locked. Still hearing the cries, they kicked in the window to discover the whole interior in flames. Anyone inside would certainly have met a horrible death. All inquiries failed to substantiate the rumor.[7]

The fire department arrived after pulling the chemical engine and hose jumpers to the scene from the station some distance away. The men arrived nearly exhausted to discover that the fire was too far away from a source of the town's water. They worked arduously to salvage anything possible, but the rapid spread and intensity of the fire prevented them from approaching the structures. A bucket brigade was formed only after the last building had burned. The *Sarasota Times* reported, "Fiercely and steadily the flames roared, the supports gave way, the buildings fell, the heavy timbers dropped into the waters with a seething hiss, and only blackened piers remain to mark the location of Sarasota's most prosperous fishing industry."[8]

On August 9, 1912, an alarm of fire was sounded again, and the department responded to Jerry Wesley Harvey's blacksmith shop. Pistol shots, whistles, and bells interrupted the usual background sound of mullet jumping in the bay as the town awoke with a start. The two-story wood structure burned like a torch, quickly consuming the materials and tools of Mr. Harvey's trade. Ironically, the hand-drawn hook and ladder truck purchased by the department was constructed in this shop only one year before.[9]

The firefighters launched their attack using the chemical engine and hose jumpers. The water available from two nearby hydrants soon quenched the fire. Not only were they successful in preventing the spread of fire to other structures, but they were also able to extinguish the fire, thus leaving the side walls and front standing.[10]

Mr. R.T. Rutherford's concern about his house was quite obvious, since his wood home on the adjacent lot appeared to be in great danger. He enlisted the help of the volunteers to help carry all of his furniture out of his house. After containing the fire, they carried it all back in and put it in place. Mr. Rutherford wanted to show his appreciation and offered to treat the entire force to dinner at the hotel of their choice. They unanimously voted for the Sarasota Cafe.[11]

The *Sarasota Times* stated, "The splendid work done by the volunteer fire department has been spoken of in terms of the highest commendation; and the force of the water from the hydrants proves that Sarasota has very effective fire protection." Mr. Harvey stated that "he will probably rebuild on the same location, but will put up a fire-proof building."[12]

Hose drying rack used to drain and dry fire hose. Constructed in 1913 behind Sarasota's first fire station, this rack looked like a giant toboggan run.

CHAPTER 10

RULES AND REGULATIONS

The fire department was organized under a military-style structure. Like the military, the fire department had a definite rank structure. The chief was in command, and the firefighters followed his orders. The fire department also maintained strict discipline to ensure order in the midst of a fire. A fireman who failed to carry out an order could endanger the lives of citizens or fellow firemen.

In order to maintain the desired level of discipline and efficiency, Chief Behrens adopted rules and regulations consisting of sixty sections. These rules and regulations, adopted by the department on July 15, 1912, became a

Sarasota Volunteer Fire Company in March 1915. Top row left to right: Irvin Riorseth, Cy Byrd, Leonard Rudd, Bill Adams, Valley Hill, Ben Hill, Hollis Bacon. Bottom row: George Willis, Henry Behrens (Chief), Ben Seale, Arnold, Jessie Hill, Myron Spencer, Rube Hayes, Frank Roberts.

standard for governing the fire department.[1]

The rules specified that the department shall consist of twelve active members, six shall be subject to first alarms and six held in reserve to respond as needed. Each man was assigned a coat called a slicker and a fireman's cap bearing the insignia of the department. Each member was compensated two dollars for responding to an alarm and performing his firefighting duties. The fire chief received five dollars. Members were paid twenty-five cents an hour for other work required for the good of the department, such as apparatus maintenance.[2,3]

Members were required to maintain proficiency with all equipment by participating in training drills at least twice a month. Firemen learned to direct fire streams to properly extinguish the fire, and to keep water damage to a minimum. Chief Behrens performed monthly inspections of the department ensuring the proficiency of the members in the various phases of firefighting.[4]

In addition to training, members had periodic duties that were specified in the rules and regulations. For instance, fire apparatus were required to be tested annually, and all fire hydrants were to be inspected monthly. Members were required to familiarize themselves with the buildings in their neighborhood in order to improve the firemen's efficiency should they be called upon to fight a fire in those buildings. Schools and all public buildings were to be inspected monthly, and a written report filed.[5]

Insubordination was handled very straightforwardly. "Members who refuse to drill, are disobedient at fires, or purposely absent themselves from duty shall be suspended for one month for the first offence and discharged for the second offense." Members found to be intoxicated at the fire station or at fires were immediately discharged. Of course, any member had the right to appeal any departmental decisions or dismissal. They could take their disagreement to the fire chief. Of course, these grievances generally did little good since the chief made the decision in the first place.[6]

CHAPTER 11

THE TURBULENT TEENS

The years between the department's inception in 1911 and the roaring twenties were very turbulent years. The department was faced with a multitude of fires that would challenge even today's departments. Still operating with hand drawn apparatus, the courageous firemen met the challenge head on.

Some Sarasotans could still vividly recall the fierceness with which the Bay View House burned in 1910. Mr. and Mrs. Hunton capitalized on the local folks' fond memories of the old structure when they constructed a new hotel and named it, the Bay View Hotel. The Hunton's completed their 30 room hotel located on Mango Avenue in 1911.[1]

Unfortunately, the Bay View Hotel met the same fate as its predecessor, the Bay View House. The alarm of fire rang out, and the flames scorched the night sky as the Bay View Hotel was steadily consumed by fire on January 18, 1913. An anxious town watched as the firemen worked to overcome first a delay in reaching the scene and then a lack of water pressure due to trouble with the tank on the hand drawn engine. Once these problems were overcome, the firemen did some good work in saving the adjoining building of Mr. Frank Higel.[2]

The hand-drawn ladder wagon was expeditiously put to use to rescue Mr. Hunton who was sleeping upstairs. He was dazed after being awakened by the smoke from the burning stairs. The men rescued him through the window by ladder to the cheers of half the town. The remainder of the family and guests were able to escape unassisted. The building was totally destroyed, but the owners intended to rebuild, this time, using concrete and brick.[3,4]

The old Dancy Building located east of the post office on Main Street burned a year later on Monday morning, January 5, 1914. Two brothers named Sessions slept over the market and narrowly escaped with their lives after heeding the panicked shouts of Mrs. Calhoun. They immediately exited from the room full of black, choking smoke as the flames burst in from the rear. The fire was believed to have been started by someone carelessly discarding a match in combustible packing material in the rear of the store. The flames found a storage of kerosene and rapidly advanced through the wood building. When the flames advanced the town watched a spectacular show as the store's supply of fireworks ignited, sending rockets, roman candles, and pinwheels skyward.[5]

Volunteers Leonard Rudd, George Lambert, and Valley Hill gallantly battled sheets of flame from the east parapet of the building where they were perched. They continued directing their hose streams down into the inferno as spectators backed away to gain relief from the heat. Simultaneously, Chief Behrens led the remainder of the department in the fight on the ground.[6]

The Sarasota Times wrote, "Sarasota is fortunate in having a most capable, level-headed executive in Chief Behrens who is supported by a volunteer force of men who work with zeal and devotion to duty." The town was forced to notice, however, the need for additional firefighting apparatus and improvements to the water supply.[7]

Annual banquet of the Sarasota Fire Department hosted by the Watrous Hotel. The menu included clam chowder, broiled pompano, roast stuffed veal, cranberry jelly, roast leg lamb, mint sauce, cold boiled ham, creamed carrots, mashed potatoes, green peas, walnut ice cream, peach shortcake and cream.

Fires became more numerous as the city continued to grow. The volunteers found it difficult to keep pace using the original hand-drawn equipment that they had purchased only three years before. Residents who had cheered before were obviously annoyed at the department's equipment shortcomings. They expressed their displeasure in the *Sarasota Times* after ex-councilman H. K. Browning's home was destroyed by fire on March 2, 1914. "By the time the hose reels were hauled eight blocks by hand there was little left worth trying to save, and as usual the fireman were almost exhausted by their exertions in getting to the scene." To the delight of the firemen, the citizens demanded that the town purchase a "motor truck." The fact that Mr. and Mrs. Browning were barely able to escape with their two partially clothed children provided the fuel for the political fire that resulted in the purchase of motorized apparatus.[8]

CHAPTER 12

HORSEPOWER WITHOUT A HORSE

Chief Behrens, accompanied by the city fathers, traveled to Tampa to witness tests of motorized fire apparatus. One of the auto trucks made a one mile run, connected to a fire plug, and pumped water in an astounding two minutes. Nothing else needed to be shown; Sarasota had to have one at once.[1]

The town council unanimously voted to purchase a motorized fire truck from the American La France Fire Engine Company. They also approved the purchase of 1000 feet of Red Cross fire hose from the Eureka Fire Hose Manufacturing Company. The mayor and town council felt the $9,000 price tag was an acceptable price for protection against the devastating effects of a conflagration. Many other cities have suffered disastrous losses and Sarasota had tasted the potential of the fire threat.[2,3]

Sarasota's new engine was the latest design manu-factured by American La France. It was as modern as any possessed by any city of its size in Florida. The combination pump and hose auto truck weighed five tons but packed speeds of 60 miles an hour. It came equipped with a 40 gallon chemical tank with 200 feet of hose and pumped 750 gallons a minute at a pressure of 200 p.s.i.. The company boasted that the truck would be able to throw a stream of water 120 feet over a building. The decision was also made to use bronze instead of cast iron in the construction of the pump to allow the fire laddies to pump salt water from the bay. This feature could have proved effective in battling the fish house fire of 1912. The engine would be able to carry a crew of eight as well as 1200 feet of two and one-half inch diameter hose and 70 feet of ladders.[4,5]

Arrangements were made immediately to enlarge the firehouse to accommodate the new engine. The

Sarasota's first motorized fire truck was a 1915 American La France engine. The structure to the right was the fire station at Pineapple and Lemon Avenues.

American La France company agreed to provide delivery from their Atlanta location in May, and the town awaited anxiously.[6]

Prior to the delivery of their new engine, Sarasota suffered a disastrous fire of a magnitude previously unrealized. The town would long remember the feeling of helplessness and the fury of the fire, that marched unrestrained down and across Main Street. The fire was discovered at 2:00 am on March 8, 1915.[7]

The fire began in the shoe-fixery shop in the rear of the five and ten cent store. The store was a part of the Lord's Building at the corner of Main Street and Pineapple Avenue. A container of some in-flammable liquid like kerosene had burst spreading flames over the floor. Fire leaped up the open stairwell as if it were a chimney. The flames' hunger for oxygen was satisfied by a draft that entered the hallway through an open door.[8]

The Tonnelier Building was considered fireproof because its exterior walls were constructed of brick. The 1912 structure contained the 38 room Palms Hotel, Palms Theater, and Palms Cafe.

The firemen and townsfolk were quick to assist those trapped on the second floor by the rapidly approaching flames. As the flames licked at both the victims and the rescuers, efforts were hastened to save those in peril. During the rescue attempt, Mrs. Willis fell from the second floor to the sidewalk below and was seriously injured. Mrs. Quigley was painfully injured when her foot struck a hook on the side of the building. Dr. Jack Halton treated the injured at the Sarasota Hotel, which served as a temporary hospital since his own office was also destroyed by the fire. Dr. Halton was also kept busy removing cinders from the firemens' eyes and dressing their burns.[9]

Flames broke through the roof of the Lord's building and battered the Tonnelier building. The three story structure of 100 x 150 feet could not withstand the attack. The brick-fortified walls did little to slow the progress of the fire as it broke through the windows and made rapid headway. Fifty-three guests who occu-

pied the Palms Hotel were evacuated from the first and second floor. Most had time to save their possessions. The proprietors, T. and L. Costello, who had leased and fully refurnished the establishment only one month before, escaped with only their nightclothes. The Palms Theatre, the Western Union Telegraph office, Dr. Joseph Halton's offices, the Crescent Pharmacy, Krebbiel's Barber Shop, and Mrs. E. L. Frazier's Bakery, which were all located on the first floor, were destroyed.[10]

Fire enveloped the entire Tonnelier block. The intense heat shattered the windows of the Gillespie Building, the First National Bank, and J. Claude Turner's store. Firemen and every able-bodied citizen worked together to try to save these buildings and the remainder of the town. They scaled their way to the rooftops to extinguish the many secondary fires that ignited. They also played streams of water on the front of the buildings to cool them. Fortunately, these buildings had fire-proof exteriors. Wood frame buildings certainly would have perished.[11]

Strong winds drove the flames like a torch toward the two-story Iwerson Block which had a full 100 foot frontage on Main Street. Fortunately it lacked windows on the side of the fire's advance, and to the builder's credit, had solid walls of concrete stone. The firemen had little hope of saving the Iwerson Block, however, because of the fierceness of the fire and the intensity of the heat. The proprietors, who occupied the Iwerson Block, including the staff of the Sarasota Times, worked feverishly to evacuate their possesions. Every available hand pitched in to make short work of it. The Sarasota Times presses were too heavy to be moved, but the fire spared them and the Iwerson Block as well.[12]

Survivors of the fire recall the fear and confusion that predominated that night. The story is still told of an individual who recklessly raced to the second floor to salvage anything in the fire's path. He intended to save an expensive typewriter, but in his panic and haste, he hurled the typewriter out the window only to have it crash on the sidewalk. He then carried a trash can of office incidentals down the stairs with all the care that would be afforded a newborn baby.[13]

During the huge fire the firemen seemingly could do little to change the sequence of events. Their hand-drawn apparatus was not capable of producing the needed fire

COURTESY JOSEPHINE WENSEL

The Tonnelier Building was razed by a devastating fire that threatened to destroy much of the Main Street business district. The 1915 fire caused $100,000 in damages. Ironically, Sarasota's first motorized fire truck had already been ordered and arrived less than two months after the Tonnelier Building burned. This fire, Sarasota's largest to date, reminded the town that uncontrolled fire threatened the citizens as well as property since two citizens were seriously injured.

The Sarasota Volunteer Fire Company pose with their new 1915 American LaFrance Engine. Chief Henry Behrens is driving. In the background is the Bank of Sarasota. The structure ultimately was remodeled into the Liggett Drug Store, which burned on April 1, 1979.

Horse power rapidly replaced manpower. The American La France engine was used to pull the ladder truck previously pulled by the volunteers.

streams, and Chief Behrens was out of town. The Bradentown Fire Department was contacted by telephone for assistance. Their arrival brought cheers, even though the fire had subsided by that time. They did, however, relieve the locals for a well deserved rest. Every Sarasota fireman had his clothing and shoes burned, and most of the men suffered blisters from the heat. All were exhausted. The Bradentown firemen quickly discovered, however, that they were unable to use Sarasota's hydrants with their hose. The threads on Sarasota's hydrants and hose used Underwriter's standard thread which was incompatible with the two and one-half inch iron pipe thread used by Bradentown.[14]

Throughout the fire the large Iwerson Building remained unscathed except for some fallen bricks and

water damage. By daybreak, however, the fire had cost the town $100,000 in lost property. Much of the damage was not insured, and several businesses closed their doors forever.[15]

Sarasota breathed a sigh of relief when its new fire engine arrived. When it was officially installed on May 1, 1915, the town turned out to admire the machine, the likes of which most have never seen before. Its sleek black chassis and nickel-plated fixtures glistened in the sun as the firemen boasted over the new symbol of their vocation.[16,17]

Many were astonished that the engine boasted 105 horsepower. Not bad for a fire department that never owned a horse! This beauty was the 793rd of its kind produced by American La France. The American La France expert arrived from Elmeria, N.Y. to demonstrate and test the department's newest acquisition.[18,19]

The town council approved the hiring of a "competent man" as driver of the fire truck. Consequently, Henry Behrens, the official chief of the volunteer fire department, was employed at a salary of seventy-five dollars per month. He became the fire department's first paid employee and commenced work on the 15th day of May in 1915. Behrens also performed the duties of night watchman.[20,21]

The town poured out to watch as Chief Behrens was instructed in its operation when the engine was

American La France engine in front of Sarasota High School. Its rotary gear pump produced 750 gal. of water per minute at 120 p.s.i. Its dual rear wheels were chain driven by a six cylinder, four cycle gasoline engine.

A triple combination pumper. The new engine carried 60 feet of ladders, 1500 feet of 2½ inch hose, and a water tank. Weighing 9,500 pounds, it was equipped with "Dayton Airless" tires.

vigorously tested to see if it would measure up to the company's claims. The engine passed with flying colors. The only hint of trouble was when one section of "Red Cross" fire hose burst, spewing water into

Mango and Eleventh street was discovered to be on fire at 2:00 a.m. on June 1, 1915. The engine responded in minutes and arrived to find the fire breaking out of the first floor windows of the two story building. Connections were made to a nearby hydrant and the heavy stream of water doused the fire. The fire was out within three minutes and the city had realized a return on their investment. The *Sarasota Times* wrote, "Chief Behrens and the fire laddies are being congratulated on their speedy work and the fire apparatus first trial was very satisfactory to the council and citizens."[23]

The city's new engine was again put to the test. The livery stable on Ninth Street (currently Third Street) owned by A.B. Edwards caught fire. The fire occurred on Tuesday afternoon on April 25, 1916. The fire destroyed the stable, but the *Sarasota Times* reported the loss as light because only one structure was destroyed.[24]

Edward's livery stable was consumed by fire on April 25, 1916. The fire department confined the fire to the stable.

the street. The annoyance was quickly replaced and the test continued. The pump, exceeded its rating of 750 gallons per minute, pumping 905 gallons per minute with little effort. Henry Behrens wrote in his test summary "I would recommend the acceptance of this pumper as it has stood all tests with a wide margin of safety."[22]

Only one month after delivery, the new engine was put to a real-world test. Milton's store at the corner of

Sarasota's motorized fire engine had proven itself well for several years. Its speed and efficiency were unquestionably superior to the hand-drawn equipment. Consequently, the city council voted to advance Chief Behrens $300 to purchase an automobile that could be used for fighting fires. The money was to be reimbursed at a rate of $25 a month from his paycheck of $75 a month. Behrens had driven a manufacturer's demonstration model brought to town by Peter Pirsch

Chief Behrens and his fire laddies were honored by leading the first Sara De Soto parade in 1916.

COURTESY JOSEPHINE WENSEL

and Sons Company in 1918 and made up his mind. When the dust had settled, the city had decided to purchase a model "White" chief's car from Peter Pirsch and Sons Co. in Kenosha, Wisconsin. This beauty carried a price tag of $2,350. Behren's and his wife drove the car home from Kenosha, Wisconsin themselves.[25,26,27,28]

The "White" passed all tests with a safe margin and was officially installed September 5, 1920. It carried a manufacturer's number of 327 and boasted a six-cylinder engine packing 60 H.P. It easily pumped its rated capacity of 350 gallons per minute. A chemical tank was added in August of 1921. The department was justifiably proud of their fleet of motorized fire engines — both of them.[29,30]

At their regular meeting on March 21, 1921, the City Council voted to advertise for sale their hand-drawn firefighting equipment. In just ten years it had become antiquated with the advent of the motorized fire engine.[31]

The fire department led the parade of the Sara De Soto Pageant on March 21, 1916. Sara De Soto was the fictitious daughter of Hernando De Soto. She was according to legend buried at sea in Sarasota Bay.

COURTESY SARASOTA COUNTY DEPARTMENT OF HISTORICAL RESOURCES

Parades were family events. This little darling managed to hitchhike a ride long enough for a photo to be taken in front of the Bank of Sarasota during the 1916 Sara De Soto parade.

COURTESY SARASOTA COUNTY DEPARTMENT OF HISTORICAL RESOURCES

Model White Chief's car was purchased for Chief Behren's use. Behrens and his wife took a train to Kenosha, Wisconsin and returned driving the White. Behrens (right) and driver (left) pose in front of the Bank of Sarasota. The White was equipped with a double action piston pump and would soon be equipped with a chemical tank.

COURTESY JOSEPHINE WENSEL

Sarasota's first fire station was enlarged in 1920 to hold the motorized fire apparatus. Left to right: 1911 hand drawn ladder truck, 1920 White chief's car, 1915 American La France.

Ladder truck in tow by the White. The American La France is shown on right. The photograph was taken behind Sarasota's first fire station.

A Champion chemical tank for firefighting was added to the White. It contained sixteen pounds bicarbonate of soda dissolved in forty gallons of water. Eight pounds sulfuric acid was mixed when necessary, causing an immediate reaction and pressure buildup that propelled the water through the fire hose.

COURTESY SARASOTA COUNTY DEPARTMENT
OF HISTORICAL RESOURCES

A rainy Armistice Day Parade in 1920. Henry Behrens drove the White on Main Street from the Hover Arcade toward Five Points. He was followed by the American La France.

COURTESY SARASOTA COUNTY DEPARTMENT
OF HISTORICAL RESOURCES

More rain fell than spectators showed for this 1920 Armistice Day Parade. Firemen drive the American La France down Main Street.

COURTESY SARASOTA COUNTY DEPARTMENT
OF HISTORICAL RESOURCES

Chapter 13

Stormy Weather

In 1921 Henry Behrens and the fire department experienced some stormy weather politically. The recent cold weather had made it necessary to tow the fire truck out of the station and crank the engine every evening. Otherwise, the engine may not start when needed. The cranking of the trucks made such a noise that several citizens began to grumble.[1]

The city council reacted to the citizens' request and passed an order that prohibited the cranking of the engines after 6:00 pm. Yet Chief Behrens continued his practice of warming the engines in defiance of the city council. He felt an overriding obligation to ensure the welfare of the town against fire. This disobedience aroused the ire of Councilman McFarland, who was also chairman of the fire committee of the council.[2,3]

The issue soon became personal. After a brief shouting match, Councilman McFarland introduced a motion calling for the "dispensing with the services of Mr. Behrens as chief of the fire department." The motion was seconded by Mr. Archibald and carried. Chief Behrens was discharged on the 21st of February in 1921.[4,5]

In his own defense Chief Behrens published the following article in the *Sarasota Times*:

An Explanation from Chief of Fire Dept.

During the latter part of the past week, it became necessary to tow the fire truck out of the fire station three times, in order to start it, and this has raised a question in the minds of a number of citizens, causing them to ask questions which I wish to answer in justice to myself.

At a recent meeting of the council an order was adopted prohibiting me from cranking the motor on the fire engines after 6 o'clock at night. As a result the engines get cold during the night and it is impossible to start them without towing them. As long as this order kept in force and the weather is cool, the starting of the motor on the fire truck will be problematical and would result in serious damage in case of a fire.

Henry Behrens,
Chief, Fire Dept.,
Sarasota, Fla.[6]

Behrens was rehired by the town council in 1928 after many of its members had changed over the years. At that time he served as the night chief of police.[7]

The appointment of a new fire chief on February 25, 1921 began a new era for the fire department. Clarence I. Stephens filled the vacancy created by Behrens's dismissal, making Stephens the department's second fire chief. Stephens salary was fixed at $125 per month, $50 more than Behrens's. Chief Stephens had previously served as assistant chief of Clearwater and Bradentown and came highly recommended. Stephens immediately reorganized the department and assigned his personnel into two fire companies: "C.I. Stephens, Chief; Geo. Landon, Assistant Chief; Dewey Maus, E. Bright, Lyman Biorseth,

Firemen pose in front of the fire station located within City Hall at the foot of Main Street.

and Richard Halton as volunteers; Erwin Gremli, Assistant Chief; and Homer Hebb, Calvin Hodges, Mason Hunt, Frank Maltby and J.W. McCarter as volunteers."[8,9,10]

In addition to testing and maintaining fire hydrants and firefighting, Chief Stephens was granted special police powers to enforce the traffic laws of the city. He received a motorcycle to chase a new town menace: speedsters and those who insisted on driving through the business district with open cutouts. The noise created by autoists who insisted on opening their cutouts bitterly angered local residents. The town was depending on Chief Stephens to abate this nuisance.[11]

The city council wanted the fire chief available for immediate response to fires at all times. What better way to obtain a rapid response than to have the fire chief live in the station? The city council made this agreement a provision when hiring Chief Stephens. The original fire station was not habitable, so provisions were made to move the fire department into the Hover Arcade at lower Main Street.[12]

The Hover Arcade was the creation of Dr. W.E. Hover and his two brothers from Ohio. They purchased the pier located at the foot of Main Street for $5,000.

The Hover Arcade was purchased for use as Sarasota's City Hall in 1917. The Fire Department moved into the building in May of 1921, replacing the original fire station at Pineapple and Lemon Avenues. The building was opened up on the left side to create a door for fire apparatus.

They extended the pier and built the Hover Arcade at its entrance in 1913 at a cost of $20,000. The original plans for the Arcade included a moving picture theatre on one wing and Dave Broadway's restaurant and ice cream parlor on the opposite wing.[13]

The building was exquisitely unique, and its archway provided both an entrance to the city pier and a gateway to the city. The Hover Arcade became the subject of many photographs and convinced northern investors that Sarasota was indeed a modern and pros-

Gateway to paradise. View looking through brick archway of the Hover Arcade towards the Palmer Bank at Five Points.

COURTESY SARASOTA COUNTY DEPARTMENT OF HISTORICAL RESOURCES

perous city. Folks frequented the arcade to catch the latest movie or to enjoy a fine meal. The childrens' eyes beamed at the thought of visiting the ice cream parlor. In 1917 the city paid $40,000 to purchase the Arcade for use as a City Hall.[14,15]

COURTESY GEORGE I. (PETE) ESTHUS, SARASOTA LOCK AND KEY SHOP

The fire department continued to occupy a portion of the City Hall building until 1935. The sign above large door on the left reads "Fire Department."

In early May 1921 Chief Stephens moved the fire department into the Hover Arcade, occupying the wing that previously held the movie theatre. The city had spent $800 in renovations to accommodate the move. The second floor housed Chief Stephens, his wife Dell, and his children. Sleeping quarters were created for the volunteers. When an alarm sounded, no time was wasted as the volunteers slid down the brass fireman's pole to the ground floor, which housed the apparatus. Stephens would be available to respond 24 hours a day, seven days a week. The small archways on the face of the south wing were modified to allow for the housing of the fire equipment. The fire department found their new quarters a vast improvement over the smaller Pineapple Avenue station.[16,17,18,19]

Sarasota continued to grow and prosper. The 1921 City Directory lists the estimated population at 3,000. The increase in growth was accompanied by an increased resentment that Sarasotans had to travel north to Bradentown to conduct much of their governmental business. Sarasotans wanted to govern themselves. Their desire for autonomy resulted in the creation of Sarasota County on July 1, 1921.[20,21,22]

The event was heralded as a triumph to a youthful but prosperous city. The entire city turned out for a parade, which marched down Main Street and through the town. The parade began a hoopla celebration that for some went on for days. "When Sarasota became a county in 1921, every fire engine rang all night because the people were so happy," recalled Reaves Wilson. Fireworks, pistol shots, and people shouting and dancing in the streets made for quite a memorable occasion.[23]

Sarasota weathered more than just political storms. Sarasota was seemingly in the tranquil waters of the political tides. Politics, however, could not begin to match the fury that Mother Nature mustered. Driving winds in excess of 80 miles per hour and pounding waves battered the city relentlessly. Many businesses were completely washed away by the no-name hurricane that blew into town on October 25, 1921. Much of the town was damaged, and the shoreline was devastated. The fire department was thankful for the sturdy brick construction of the Hover Arcade, which weathered the storm with little trouble.[24]

The city pier was not so fortunate. Most of the pier was swept away along with most of the fish houses. The remains of a thriving industry littered the shoreline of Gulfstream Avenue. The city, however, turned problems into opportunities when they rebuilt

The fire department led the parade as Sarasota officially became a county on July 1, 1921. The grand celebration continued for days.

Gulfstream Avenue was littered with the wreckage from the wood Municipal Pier and the local fishing industry. Fortunately, the Arcade Building and the Fire Department weathered the winds, which exceeded 80 mph when the hurricane struck Sarasota on October 25, 1921.

the municipal pier out of concrete and relocated the smelly and unsightly fish houses to Hogs Creek, a location north of the pier.[25]

The sun set on Clarence I. Stephens reign as fire chief in 1924. Sarasota was about to experience a period of new growth that began with a new fire chief.[26]

CHAPTER 14

FEAST TO FAMINE

During the 1920's Sarasota experienced unprecedented growth. New construction moved forward and was out paced only by the numbers of realtors and investors seeking to make quick fortunes from property sales. Sarasota's population had increased dramatically and by 1925, the city boasted 5,529 residents. The First Bank and Trust Company began construction of their new skyscraper at the northeast corner of Five Points in 1924 and is still standing today. In the years to follow, many Sarasota landmarks were erected. The Mira Mar Casino and the John Ringling Causeway were constructed in 1925. The El Verona (currently the John Ringling Towers), the Sarasota County Courthouse and the Edwards

The El Verona was constructed in 1926 by Owen Burns and named after his wife. John Ringling, the circus magnate, purchased the building and renamed it John Ringling Hotel. The John Ringling Hotel was without question the most elite hotel in Sarasota. It was acquired from the Ringling estate by the Arvida Corporation. Later, H.W. Robinson purchased the building, remodeled it into apartments, and reopened it in 1964 as the Ringling Towers. The Ringling Towers at the time of this publication stands vacant and badly deteriorated. Its Spanish architecture stands out as a shadow of Sarasota's past. An effort is currently underway to restore the building to its previous splendor.

Theatre, now the Sarasota Opera House were constructed in 1926.[1,2]

In contrast, some parts of Florida were not equally blessed. After World War I, the United States Navy returned to normalcy and greatly reduced the massive buildup that had occurred to meet the demands of the war. After 1919, the demand for personnel, equipment, and supplies had all but vanished. Many of the civilians who supported the Key West naval operation, therefore, saw the writing on the wall and departed. One of those individuals was Harry Maitland Knowles.[3]

Knowles was born in Key West to Rosie and David Knowles on October 1, 1893. Due to his father's illness, he left school at age ten to help support his mother and father. He found employment working as a messenger boy for the Florida East Coast Railroad during the time they extended the line from Miami to Key West. He worked for the railroad for eight years but also obtained a chief engineers license to pilot a boat. Knowles was employed by the Key West Fire Department as assistant chief in 1914, and served as the superintendent of vehicles at the United States Navy Yard in Key West in 1917. Knowles moved to Tarpon Springs when the military activity began to dwindle in Key West during peacetime. He was employed by the Cowsert Bus Line, which was owned by the brother of future Sarasota Fire Chief James R. Cowsert. Knowles also became a member of the Tarpon Springs Fire Department and eventually was promoted to chief.[4,5,6]

Harry Maitland Knowles moved to Sarasota in 1923 to accept a job as chief engineer on one of the Ringling yachts. When he arrived here, he discovered that Sarasota was looking for a fire chief. Knowles opted for the job with the more permanent future and accepted the position as fire chief.[7]

Knowles was appointed as the department's third fire chief on June 1, 1924. He earned $150.00 per month, was on duty seven days a week, and was the only paid employee of the fire department. Fortunately the volunteer ranks were strong. The department still operated their two pieces of motorized fire apparatus, a 1915 American La France and a 1920 White from the Hover Arcade. Knowles was authorized by the city to hire an assistant chief. He enlisted the services of James R. Cowsert, who had worked with and befriended Knowles in Tarpon Springs.[8,9]

Sarasota's population increased steadily. New construction caused the town to bulge upward and outward. The number of emergencies answered by the

Seagrave Aerial ladder truck, 1925. The seventy-five foot wooden ladder was raised by a hand crank.

Bird's-eye view of the 1925 Seagrave Aerial.

department grew every year as did the height of the buildings. As a result, many buildings grew beyond the reach of the tallest ladder owned by the department.

Since many residents still remembered the fires in previous years that nearly destroyed the town, Chief Knowles found little resistance when he suggested the purchase of a new aerial ladder truck. A Seagrave aerial ladder truck was purchased in 1925. It contained a wooden ladder mounted to the apparatus that could reach a height of 75 feet and had solid rubber tires. It was termed a spring aerial because the ladder was raised by a spring mechanism assisted by a hand crank. The full length of the ladder was extended on November 7, 1952 while fighting a fire at the Palmer Bank Building, then valued at $262,430. The fire was on the roof so the ladder proved to be too short and of little use. The damage was kept to a minimum because of the quick action of firemen who carried their hose and equipment up the stairs and extinguished the fire.[10,11]

The purchase of the Seagrave aerial ladder truck raised the ire of Peter Pirsch, another manufacturer of fire apparatus, who lived in Sarasota. His steamy letters stated that the city's money was "fooled away" because they purchased a Seagrave instead of a Pirsch.

Sarasota's 1925 Seagrave Aerial standing in readiness.

He called for a change in city government and recommended that the city hire a city manager. Sarasota's first city manager, Ross Windom, was not hired until January of 1946, nearly twenty-one years later. Pirsch stated that with a city manager, "Big high powered influential citizens can get no closer to him than the humblest citizen so far as pulls are concerned to get a public improvement if it is for anybody's personal pecuniary benefit." Peter Pirsch's apparatus were less expensive, however, there were none operating in Florida for the city to evaluate prior to the purchase. Sarasota simply refused to buy one sight unseen.[12,13]

Sarasota purchased an additional engine from the Seagrave Company in 1926. With growth occurring at such a rapid rate it was essential that the fire department not become outpaced. Sarasota's real estate sales for the previous year tallied up to a whopping $11,420,000. This latest purchase was labeled engine number three, with the White and American La France being numbers one and two. Peter Pirsch again wrote to Mayor Bacon. This time he accused the city of "criminal" action by violat-

The 1925 Seagrave Aerial in front of the Municipal Auditorium. The auditorium held its grand opening during the Sara de Soto celebration on February 24, 1938. More than 3,000 people attended.

Sarasota's 1926 Seagrave Suburbanite engine is shown at the factory just prior to shipping to Sarasota.

ing "Uncle Sam and the Cracker State laws."[14]

Despite Pirsch's criticism, the Sarasota Fire Department achieved great results. Chief Knowles and the volunteers were honored when the *Sarasota Times* published an article declaring "Sarasota's Fire Loss Lowest of Any City in All United States." From June 1, 1924 to December 1, 1926, over 400 alarms of fire were handled. During that length of time, only $29,000 in damages occurred. The *Times* said that "this speaks volumes for our fire department and its high standard of efficiency."[15]

Beginning in 1925 the nation's thirst for Florida real estate had been quenched. Florida resort areas like Sarasota launched major advertising programs to attract potential buyers and investors. Word of mouth had already preceded the advertizing blitz, and northerners feared inflated prices, unscrupulous real estate deals, and a lack of affordable housing. When the infamous September 18 hurricane in 1926 blew through Sarasota, fierce winds battered not only buildings but any hopes of economic recovery for the near future.[16]

Late in 1926 circus magnate John Ringling made a decision that changed the character of Sarasota forever and helped the city survive the financial woes of the coming depression. Ringling chose Sarasota as his new winter circus headquarters. He purchased the fair-grounds and directly proceeded with his plans. He envisioned an open air arena where an audience could watch performers practice — for a price. Ringling said that he was going "to make Sarasota one of the sights of the South" and he did indeed. The circus train arrived with fully one hundred cars, bringing with it 1400 people to town. Its animal trainers, aerialists, cooks, beautiful young maidens, clowns, and roustabouts practically created a city within itself. It also changed the flavor of the annual Sarasota pageant by making it a grandiose event.[17]

The arrival of the circus made Chief Knowles question the fire department's ability to adequately protect the little circus city from fire. Knowles felt it necessary to purchase an additional engine. After eight years of reliable service, Knowles traded in the 1920 White for a brand new 1928 American La France Engine. The city received $2,600 credit for the White leaving a balance of $10,400. That was not a bad trade-in considering that the city did not pay that much for the White in the first place. The new engine pumped 1000 gallons per minute and represented the latest in technology.[18,19]

The fire department responded to the circus headquarters on numerous alarms. On one occasion the contents of a hay barn was burning. The firemen did some impromptu recruiting by enlisting the services of one of the Ringling elephants. The elephant removed

Sarasota Fire Department in 1929. Photo taken on the municipal pier. Chief Knowles is second from left. The structure in the distance is the El Vernona Hotel.

the unburned bales of hay from the building while the firemen worked to extinguish the fire using hose lines. This cooperative effort limited the damage to sixty bales of hay and left the barn unscathed.[20]

In spite of the boost provided by John Ringling, economic times were hard and were getting progressively worse. The city's 1928 American La France engine was repossessed by the manufacturer on December 15, 1932 because Sarasota was no longer able to make payments. During the depression Chief Knowles and Assistant Chief Cowsert took a salary cut and doubled as caretakers for City Hall and the adjoining park.[21,22]

President Roosevelt established the Federal Economic Recovery Act to provide economic relief for a financially troubled nation. One aspect of the act was to create Works Progress Administration (WPA) projects. The WPA projects served two purposes. First, they provided jobs and income for many hard-pressed families. Second, they provided needed improvements that cities otherwise could not afford. WPA funds were responsible for many improvements to Sarasota. They helped build the Municipal Auditorium in 1938, the Chidsey Library, Osprey Avenue Bridge, and the Lido Casino. The WPA funds were also used to renovate the old jail for use as a fire station.[23,24]

The Ninth Street Station was once the Sarasota County Jail. The jail which closed for security reasons, was remodeled using WPA funds into a fire station. As a result of the modern renumbering of streets, it is currently located at 1426 Third Street. The apparatus is the 1925 Seagrave Aerial.

The county commission resolved on November 4, 1935, "that county convey to city of Sarasota property on Ninth Street upon condition that said property shall be used by city exclusively as a fire station, same to revert to county when such use ceases or is discontinued by the city."[25]

The structure that later served as this fire station was originally constructed as a garage for A.B. Edwards, in 1913. Edwards, who had a sixth sense in both business and politics, constructed the building for a garage. He predicted the need for a garage for repairing the motor cars that were beginning to congest the town's streets. His vision rewarded him financially. He also became Sarasota's first mayor.[26]

The buildings first tenant was the Swain-Jay Garage Company. The building was vacated in 1917 and remained empty until sold to Sarasota County in 1922. The county used the structure as a three-cell jail beginning in 1922 but ceased in 1926 due to security deficiencies. The county leased the building to a variety of tenants for the next several years.[27]

In 1935 the city of Sarasota used federal Works Projects Administration funds to renovate the old jail into a fire station. Federal dollars and hard work were able to convert a dilapidated structure into what was

The 1925 Seagrave Aerial inside of Ninth Street Fire Station.

then a modern, functioning fire station. Before years end, the department moved into their new home at 261 W. Ninth Street, later readdressed in the year 1953 to 1426 Third Street. Paid firemen now numbered eighteen. The new station provided a more central location which was hoped would shorten response times.[28,29]

Sarasota played host to the twelfth annual convention of the Florida State Firemen's Association in 1937. The guests registered at the SaraSota Hotel and prepared for two full days of business and sightseeing led by Chief Knowles himself. After the days work, Knowles led the visit-

Firefighters in front of the Ninth Street Fire Station. Firefighters from left to right: Chief Knowles, Mose Hood, James Cowsert, John Davis, Wiley Walker, Walter Gaskill.

This photo of the fire that occurred in the condemned Mira Mar Auditorium shows the street light half blackened. This practice, which dated from WWII, was intended to keep the town hidden from German ships and subs at night. The fire occurred February 2, 1955.

War bonds were sold at Five Points with the assistance of the fire department.

ing firemen by motorcade to Lido beach and the Ringling Art Museum. They finished off the evening with a banquet of fried chicken and danced the night away at the Tin Can Tourists Camp, currently Sarasota Mobile Home Park.[30]

The 1940's brought more changes. World War II affected every fiber of America including Sarasota and its fire department. Sarasotans felt the daily impact of the conflict which was occurring thousands of miles away — or was it? Even the face of the town changed. An air base complete with barracks was constructed where the Sarasota\Bradenton Airport currently stands. B-52 bombers cast an ominous shadow on the otherwise magnificent landscape of the town as they flew overhead. On June 12, 1942 local headlines told of a B-52 bomber that crashed before dawn in the bay just south of Whitfield Estates. Eight crew members were killed and two injured. The bomber had just taken off from the Sarasota airbase. Sarasota, like other coastal towns, practiced dusk to dawn blackouts to prevent the German ships and subs from seeing the town from the water at night. The war's effect lingered long after the fighting ended. One house on Little Roberts Bay was constructed with poured concrete walls, roof-mounted searchlights to scan the bay, and an underground cistern should the water supply be poisoned. A steel-reinforced bomb shelter was added

Toys for tots. Toys donated by citizens were repaired by firefighters and given to needy children for Christmas. Posing inside the Ninth Street Station are left to right: Curtis Tucker, James Sumner, Don Hoover, Otto Manson, Bill Wagner, Rufus Fralick, and John Stone.

years later. On the positive side, thousands of service men and women passed through Sarasota and so loved the town that they returned to raise their families here after the war.[31,32]

The fire department spearheaded a drive to raise money for the war effort. They raised the seventy-five foot wooden ladder of the Seagrave aerial at Five Points to promote war bonds. A lovely Ringling Circus aerial performer climbed one rung for every twenty-five dollars worth of war bonds sold. Enough money was raised for her to go up one side and down the other.

The "Old Mac" in 1938, when it was the pride of the Department. It sported dual ignition and a pump that put out a whopping 750 gallons per minute.

Sarasota's firemen continued to wage war against fire long after the military war overseas had ended.

All was not smooth sailing fiscally for the fire department either. The city's firemen found themselves in somewhat of a predicament in 1942 that almost beat the pants off of them, literally! It seemed that the firemen were desperately in need of a dozen new pair of uniform pants. The city council adamantly refused to pay $13.75 per pair. The council finally bowed to reason and prevented the department from getting caught with their pants down.[33]

Sarasota Memorial Hospital opened its doors in its current location on November 2, 1925. By the time the 32-bed public hospital was completed, it was already too small for the growing community. The hospital expanded its capacity to 60 patient beds by 1927 and has continued to grow. By 1952 it had grown tremendously in size and importance to the community. Should there be a fire in the hospital, it was doubtful that the firemen could arrive in sufficient time from their sole station on Third Street. On June 1, 1952 the department opened the doors to their new station located just one block south of the hospital at 1821 Hillview Street.[34]

Knowles tenure as fire chief had certainly achieved numerous milestones. Probably the most significant of which was obtaining a second-class fire insurance rating from the Insurance Services Office (I.S.O.). The

Assistant Chief James Cowsert sits on the running board of the "Old Mac" with the spring aerial in the background. This photograph was taken in front of the Ninth Street Station in 1939.

The 1938 Mack, triple combination pumper. Left to right: Chief Maitland Knowles, Assistant Chief James Cowsert, Wiley Walker, Mose Hood, John Davis, Walter Gaskill.

Restoration efforts are planned at the time of this publication to restore this 1938 Mack to its original splendor. Time has taken its toll on this vintage engine.

I.S.O. was an organization that rated fire departments on a scale from one to ten and makes rate recommendations to insurance companies. The department was well respected for its second-class rating, and the citizens appreciated the savings on their insurance bills. Upon Knowles's retirement on July 1, 1952, city residents paid just 28 cents per one-hundred dollars of property value. This was in sharp contrast to the $1.09 paid by Sarasotans before Knowles was hired.[35,36]

The Hillview Fire Station served the community in many ways. The stations served as polling places for elections. October 1, 1974.

A company of firefighters assigned at the Hillview Fire Station.

CHAPTER 15

POPS

James R. Cowsert became the fourth chief of the department in January 1, 1953. He was well prepared to fill the chief's shoes when Knowles retired. After all, he had already done so. Knowles had resigned from the department January 19, 1934 and went to work for the Ringling Circus as a truck driver. At that time, Cowsert was appointed fire chief. Knowles was later rehired and reinstated as chief by the city commission, thus, forcing Cowsert to accept a demotion. Knowles again announced his retirement on April 7, 1952 upon which Cowsert became the acting chief. Cowsert became the probationary chief on July 1, 1952, and once again fire chief.[1,2]

Born in Mississippi and raised in Tarpon Springs, Cowsert spent his childhood helping his "Papa" in his many business endeavors. Papa operated a dry goods store that supplied provisions for the sponge boats that operated from Tarpon Springs. Papa later built the first motorized sponge boats, naming one of them James after his son. James helped in the dry goods store, cared for the family garden, and worked at Papa's livery stable. The livery stable had a contract to haul kerosene and gasoline for the Gulf Oil Company. James hauled the fuel in ten-gallon cans first using a horse and wagon then a Model-T Ford truck, which James used to haul cans to towns as far away as Clearwater.[3]

James Cowsert wed Catherine Edwards in Tarpon Springs and honeymooned in beautiful Sarasota. They enjoyed the pristine beaches and each others company before returning to Tarpon Springs and moving in with the Cowsert family. James's father had started a busline, which grew to be quite successful. James worked in his father's garage maintaining the buses and driving occasionally along with the future fire chief Harry Knowles. Troubles arrived when James and Catherine separated and James became ill with typhoid fever and was laid up for several months.[4]

Firefighter training is essential. Chief Cowsert personally scrutinizes this practical training session at Hog's Creek. Hog's Creek was located on the north side of Tenth Street, west of Tamiami Trail North.

James Cowsert moved to Sarasota in 1924 and was appointed assistant chief by Knowles on November 6. Cowsert, along with the rest of Sarasota, experienced the boom of the 1920's and the extremely difficult financial times that followed while working along side Knowles.[5]

Cowsert had a true love for the fire department and his firemen. They considered him almost like family. He knew every fireman's wife and children personally and stopped by their houses to visit when a family ill-

Dorothy Tuynman (center) served as the Department's first secretary. She was affectionately known as "Mother."

ness occurred. His fatherly concern for his men earned him the nickname "Pops."[6]

In spite of his friendship with the firemen, Cowsert ran a tight ship. He did not tolerate disobedience or insubordination. In fact, he once fired a man on the spot for having a beer in the station refrigerator. Dorothy Tuynman said, "It seemed that Chief Cowsert was always at the fire station. He would go home for supper and then come right back. He loved the fire department." Dorothy, affectionately known by the firemen as "Mother," was the department's sole secretary for many years. The men recollect that, "Cowsert might have been the chief, but Mother kept the place running."[7,8]

A report of a brush fire at the old circus headquarters was received on a hot summer afternoon by the fire department. The circus headquarters was located near Oriente Avenue, now Beneva Road north, and Glen Oaks Boulevard. A single engine with two firemen responded from the Fourth Street station. The remaining firemen looked to the east and watched the column of light-colored smoke diffusely rising. The firemen reported their arrival by radio and went to work. Back at the station, the firemen noticed the column of smoke turned thick and black. Nobody seemed concerned because brush fires were routine calls that time of year and generally did little harm.

Several hours had passed when the two withered firemen walked into the station carrying a fire extinguisher and a nozzle. The chief and firemen looked aghast when they heard of their drama. It seemed the fire engine was positioned to fight the brush fire in an area of unburned brush. The old International engine stalled, thus stopping the pump, and was rapidly consumed by the fire. The black column of smoke was the engine and its load of rubber hose burning. The firemen had only enough time to save themselves along with the extinguisher and nozzle. The two hitched a ride back to the station while clutching their meager trophies on their laps.

Firemen learned to attack future brushfires from the already burned side of the fire for two reasons. First, the fire is less likely to sweep over the firemen and destroy their apparatus. Second, rattlesnakes were slithering ahead of the approaching fire in an attempt to escape the heat and smoke. Early firemen carried burlap sacks on the engines and captured the serpents using their rakes. They delivered them to a local pet store and received 75 cents per foot for each rattle snake. The snakes were then used to created antivenom.

The St. Armands fire station was located to protect the residents and tourists on St. Armands Key. The station was later expanded to add a third apparatus bay.

Sarasotans, keenly aware of the dollars that the tourist trade brought in, developed many businesses on the islands west of the city. Bird Key, St. Armand's Key, and Lido Beach continued to attract Sarasotans and tourists alike. Chief Cowsert, therefore, invested $18,440 for the construction of an additional fire station at 47 North Adams Drive to better care for the northern guests and residents of the keys. When its doors opened on November 1, 1955, Sarasota's finest were ready for action. Although emergencies were few, the department was ready none the less.[9]

By 1958 Sarasota's resident population had increased to 37,500 and the number of alarms that the fire department responded to increased accordingly. In addition, Sarasota's population grew tremendously with the arrival of the annual winter tourists. In order to keep up with this increase, the city dedicated $93,000 of a 4.7 million dollar bond issue passed that same year to the construction of a new central fire station.[10,11,12]

The Main Headquarters and administrative offices of the Fire Department opened in 1960 at 1445 Fourth Street. The station also has housed a full complement of apparatus and CommCe, the Department's dispatch center.

The new fire station and administration headquarters opened its doors on January 7, 1960. The station was nearly double the size of the Third Street station which it replaced, and was constructed just one block north at 1445 Fourth Street.

The Fourth Street Station featured air-conditioned living quarters and administrative offices. The dormitory room had its twenty-four bunks strategically arranged for speedy travel to the apparatus floor. During the daytime, each bunk was crisply made with pale green blankets, which the firemen used in the evening if they were lucky.[13] The administrative offices of the department were designed for a rapidly expanding business with an even faster growing clientele. The fire department faced a multitude of challenges in addition to the mere increase in number of alarms. State and federal standards progressively became more stringent. The department gradually expanded its administrative staff to support the ongoing firefighting

efforts. The department also met the public's need for expanded services such as fire prevention education and emergency medical services.

The kitchen was another feature even closer to the hearts of the firemen since twenty-four hour shifts caused stomachs to rumble more than once. Firemen would routinely volunteer to double as cook, buying groceries from a common fund into which each man contributed. Meals were generally a time to relax and enjoy each other's fellowship. It was one of the few times when quiet would interrupt the boisterous and lighthearted comradery. Sunday brunch became a tradition that is still enjoyed today. The typical menu of eggs, bacon, sausage, pancakes, grits, toast, orange juice and coffee satisfied the heartiest of appetites. All meals, of course, were subject to interruption when duty called.

Fire station #4, located at 3530 Bradenton Road was opened January 23, 1960. It shortened response times for calls in north Sarasota.

Cowsert opened the northside fire station at 3530 Bradenton Road on January 25, 1960, thereby increasing the number of stations to four. Its construction was completed three weeks after the opening of the fire headquarters on Fourth Street and was financed under the same bond issue. Cowsert justified the need for the northside station by offering shorter response times to the north end of the city, which had a majority of the city's wood-framed structures. It also placed a station within a reasonable distance to the Ringling Museum of Art, Ringling Mansion, and other expensive northside attractions.[14]

Changes in technique and equipment also came to the department. Cowsert stated that he had, "never been seriously burned because in earlier days a man was considered a fool if he went inside a building to fight the

Fireman wearing a canister-style mask extinguishes an interior fire in a new cement block home at Twenty-Seventh Street and Pershing Avenue. The fire, which occurred on December 7, 1954, was extinguished in fifteen minutes.

flames. Back in those days, you stood outside the building and pumped water and chemicals on the blaze until it was drowned." Consequently water damage generally exceeded the damage caused by heat and smoke. The combination of the superheated atmospheres, acrid smoke, and toxic gases such as carbon monoxide prevented firemen from entering burning structures.[15]

With the arrival of the canister mask — otherwise known as the filter mask — in the 1940's, firemen were able to enter the burning structures and apply water directly on the seat of the fire thus causing less water damage. The canister masks contained a mask connected to a canister that filtered out smoke particles and carbon monoxide. The canister was used until it was hot indicating that it was expired. Canister masks

did not filter out a number of harmful and toxic gases. Canister masks were replaced by self contained breathing apparatus, beginning in 1958, which contained a 30 minute supply of compressed air.[16]

One of the most memorable fires of Cowsert's career was the West Coast Lumber blaze on January 7, 1957. The fire burned for nearly seven hours and threatened stores of lumber and nearby bulk fuel tanks. The nighttime blaze required a mutual effort by the Sarasota Fire Department and the South Trail Volunteer Fire Department to extinguish.[17]

Cowsert retired July 12, 1966 after serving the department for more than 41 years. Announcing his retirement, Cowsert said, "I doubt that I'll be able to stop myself from following a fire engine's siren."[18]

Self-contained breathing apparatus (right) were heralded as a major breakthrough for firefighter safety.

Firefighter Tom Rhoades (right) takes a moment to cool down at a training fire. May 23, 1963.

Heavy smoke pushes out the rear door of the Snack House Restaurant as firemen prepare to enter. August 26, 1962.

The 1954 Pirsch Aerial is set up on Third Street across from the fire station. Central Avenue is at left, looking west. Positioned upon the 85 foot ladder are from top to bottom: Don Hoover, John Stone, Vernon Wallers, Bill Wagner, James Sumner, Curtis W. Tucker. 1954.

Fireman Bob McLeod sits perched on the ladder of the 1954 Pirsch Aerial while applying water to extinguish a fire at the Snack House Restaurant.

Old Truck 5 overheats again. The Snack House was a popular hangout for Sarasota's youth. It was damaged by fire on August 26, 1962.

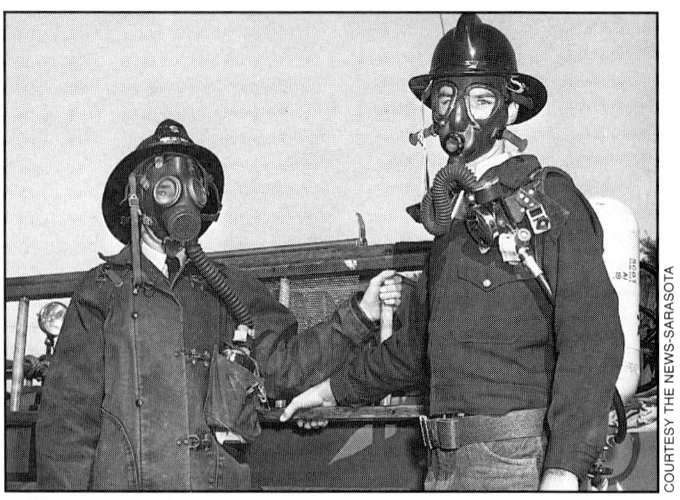

Self-contained breathing apparatus, S.C.B.A. (right), began to replace the canister style mask (left) in 1958. S.C.B.A. contained approximately 30 minutes supply of compressed air. Firemen George Rebar and William Curtis Tucker demonstrate the equipment.

(Chapter 15 continued on page 75)

Fire station #1 is located at 1445 Fourth Street. Today, it houses the department's administrative headquarters, CommCe, and a fully equipped fire company. January 1966.

Skilled Emergency Apparatus Mechanics like Larry Martini maintain department apparatus in top shape to perform lifesaving missions.

Computer-aided dispatch linked to an enhanced 9-1-1 emergency telephone system maximize the speed and accuracy of emergency dispatch in CommCe. Communications controller II's Mary Anne Hecht (left) and Ray Fisher (right) monitor emergencies currently in progress.

The Lynn Hotel Fire on July 16, 1985 resulted in the death of three civilians. Firefighters arrived to find civilians jumping from windows to escape the fire, which extensively involved the building. The fire was later determined to be caused by arson.

COURTESY SARASOTA FIRE-RESCUE. PHOTO BY DENNIS SARGENT

COURTESY SARASOTA FIRE-RESCUE

Firefighters make entry to a structure fire in a commercial building housing the Praise Doll Factory at 2123 10th Street. One firefighter was transported to Sarasota Memorial Hospital suffering from heat exhaustion. June 21, 1984.

Firefighters continue overhaul operations at the Whitesides Appliance Store at 1618 Main Street. January 3, 1986.

COURTESY SARASOTA FIRE-RESCUE. PHOTO BY DENNIS SARGENT

PHOTO BY JOHN MCCARTHY
COURTESY SARASOTA COUNTY DEPARTMENT OF HISTORICAL RESOURCES

This historic structure was occupied in 1918 by George Franklin, a previous mayor of Sarasota. The structure located on Morrill Street was built around the turn of the century and burned on December 8, 1983.

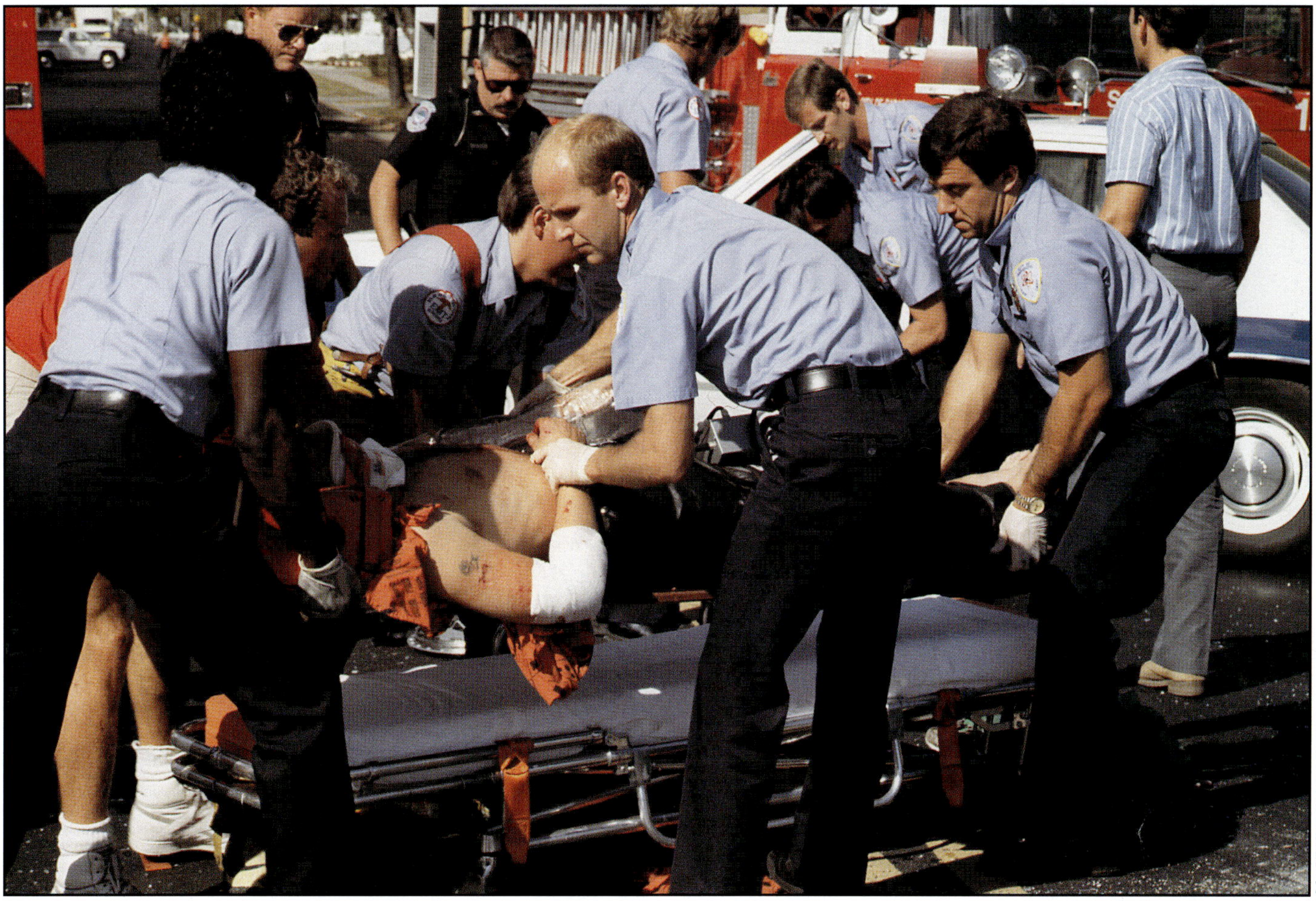

A motorcycle accident patient is loaded on a stretcher and prepared for transport.

COURTESY WAYNE A. WELSH

A young drowning victim is successfully resuscitated by paramedics Rob Chiesa and Ken Sims.

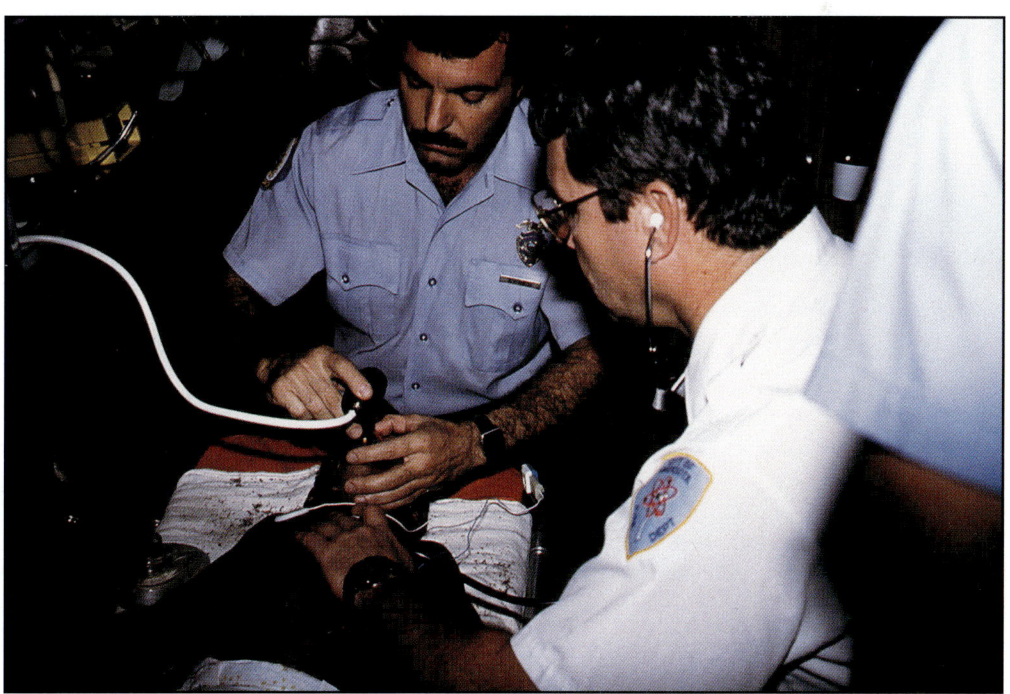

COURTESY JAMES FRAZIER
PHOTO BY JAMES FRAZIER

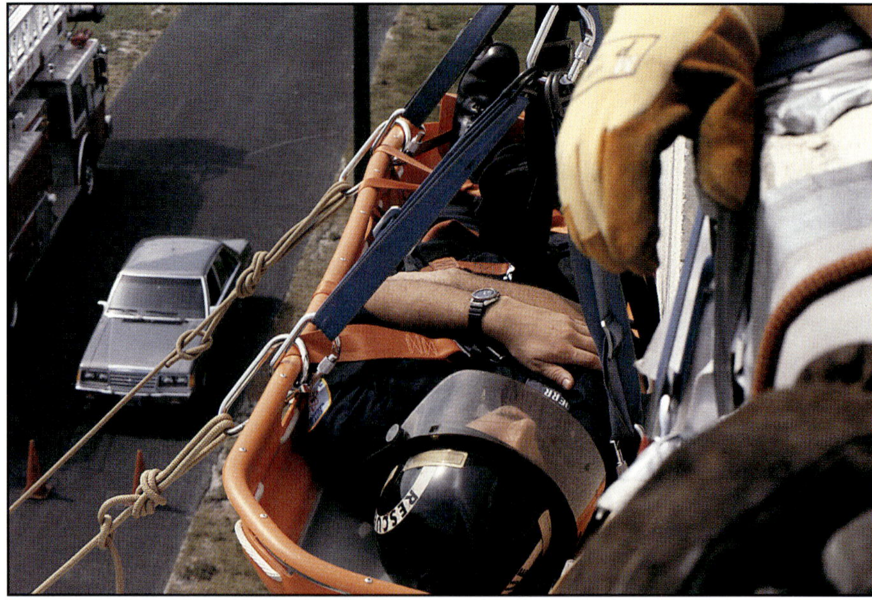

Bayflight Medical Helicopter departs the scene of a two vehicle accident enroute to Bayfront Medical Center, a level two trauma center. The helicopter bypassed Sarasota Memorial Hospital since it was not a designated trauma center.

COURTESY WAYNE A. WELSH

Firefighters literally place their lives in each others hands. A firefighter is lowered off the side of a building by his comrades in a rescue training exercise.

COURTESY SARASOTA FIRE-RESCUE

COURTESY SARASOTA FIRE-RESCUE. PHOTO BY BILL CARLIN

The parking garage collapse at Sarasota Memorial Hospital injures three workers. Firefighters search through rubble for unaccounted workers. November 17, 1981.

Two patients from a motorcycle accident receive medical assistance.

John Ringling Towers has been the victim of several fire incidents. The vacant building suffered minor damage from several small fires started by vagrants during the 1980's and early 1990's. Fire Chief Thomas Fields oversees operations.

COURTESY WAYNE A. WELSH

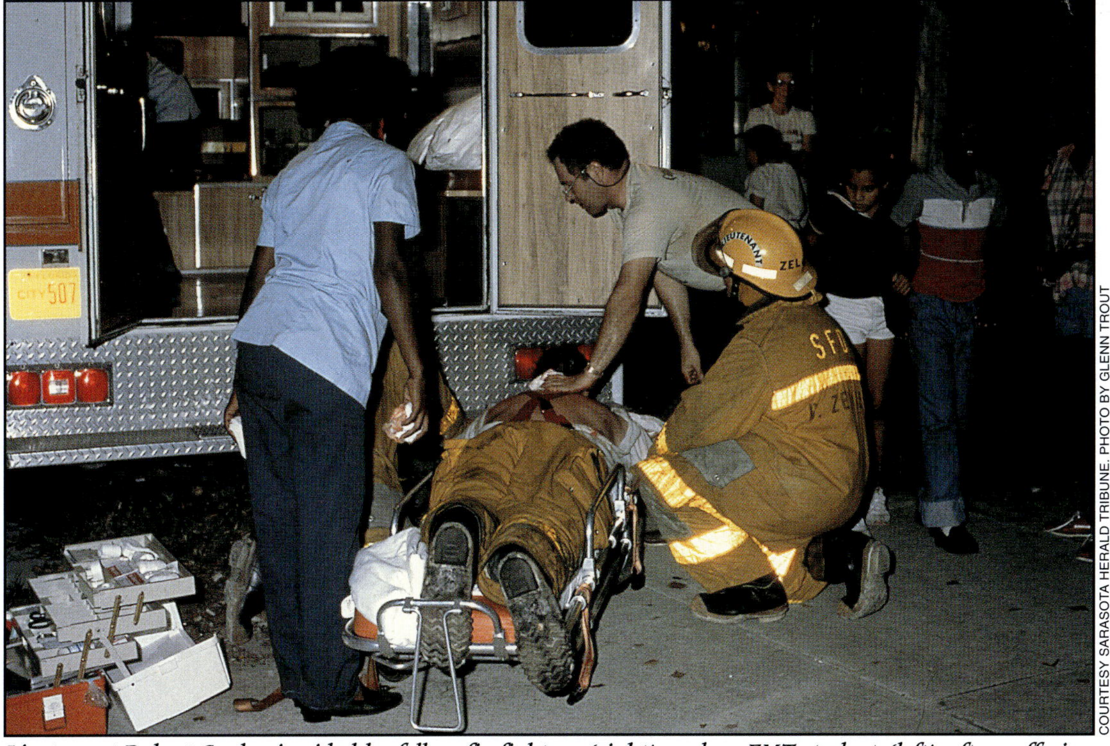

COURTESY SARASOTA HERALD TRIBUNE. PHOTO BY GLENN TROUT

Lieutenant Robert Conley is aided by fellow firefighters (right) and an EMT student (left) after suffering injuries while battling a structure fire at the Miner's Furniture Store at 1534 Third Street. November 27, 1985.

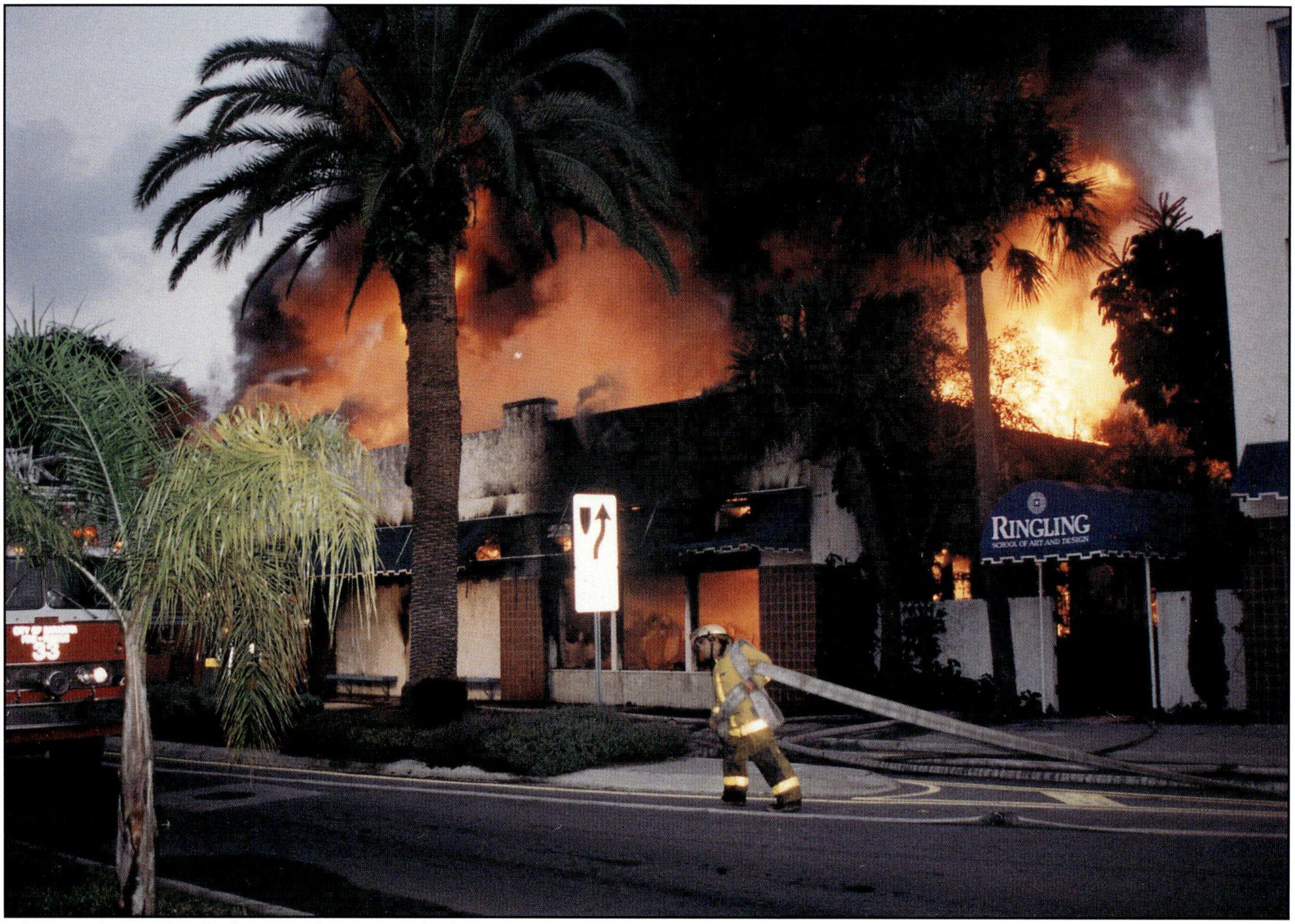

COURTESY SARASOTA FIRE-RESCUE. PHOTO BY CAPTAIN DAN THIBODEAU

The Ringling School of Art and Design which occupies the historic Bay Haven Hotel which was originally constructed in 1926. Named after the circus magnate John Ringling, it is one of the top art and design schools in the country. An early morning fire destroyed a building which was used for a student cafeteria and classrooms. August 8, 1989.

The command post at the Ringling School of Art and Design blaze directed firefighting efforts. August 8, 1989.

COURTESY SARASOTA FIRE-RESCUE
PHOTO BY CAPTAIN DAN THIBODEAU

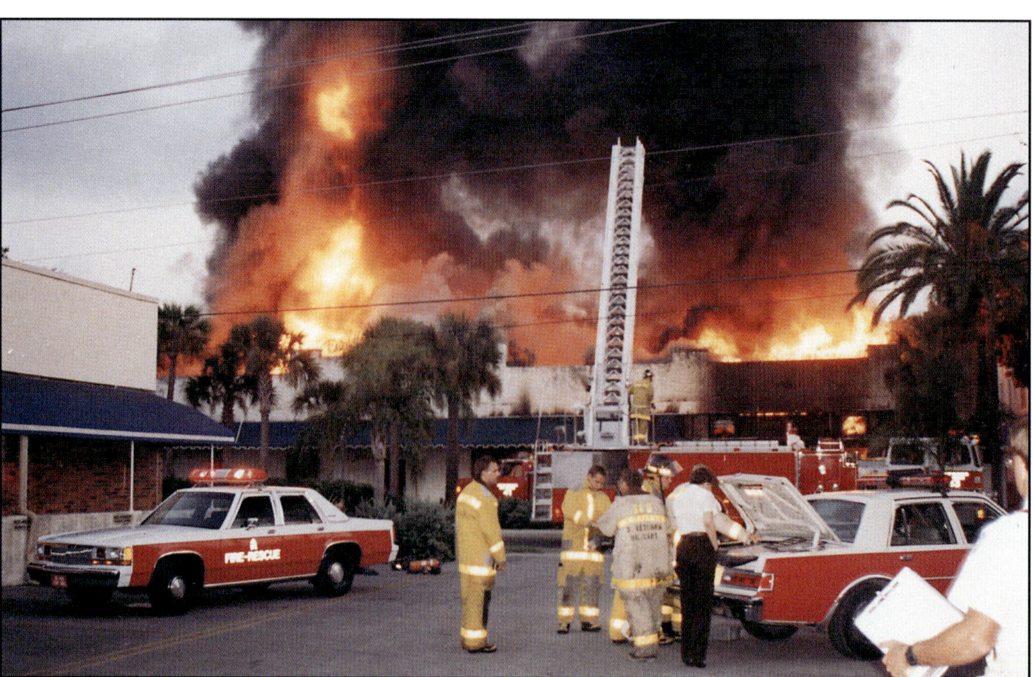

The first arriving engine at the Ringling School of Art and Design prepared to battle a difficult fire. Intense heat and a collapsing roof drove firefighters out of the structure. Firefighters confined the fire to a single building. August 8, 1989.

Firefighters take pride in their work. Gary Potter (left) and John Lawton (right) clean Engine-11, the busiest engine company in the department. March 1989.

Teamwork is an essential part of being a firefighter. Firefighters load hose on Engine-11 after testing the hose for reliability. January 1989.

A thick cloud of smoke engulfs a company of firefighters as they extinguish a flammable liquid fire.

Firefighters push back the flames using two hoselines to protect a tank of liquid petroleum gas during a training drill.

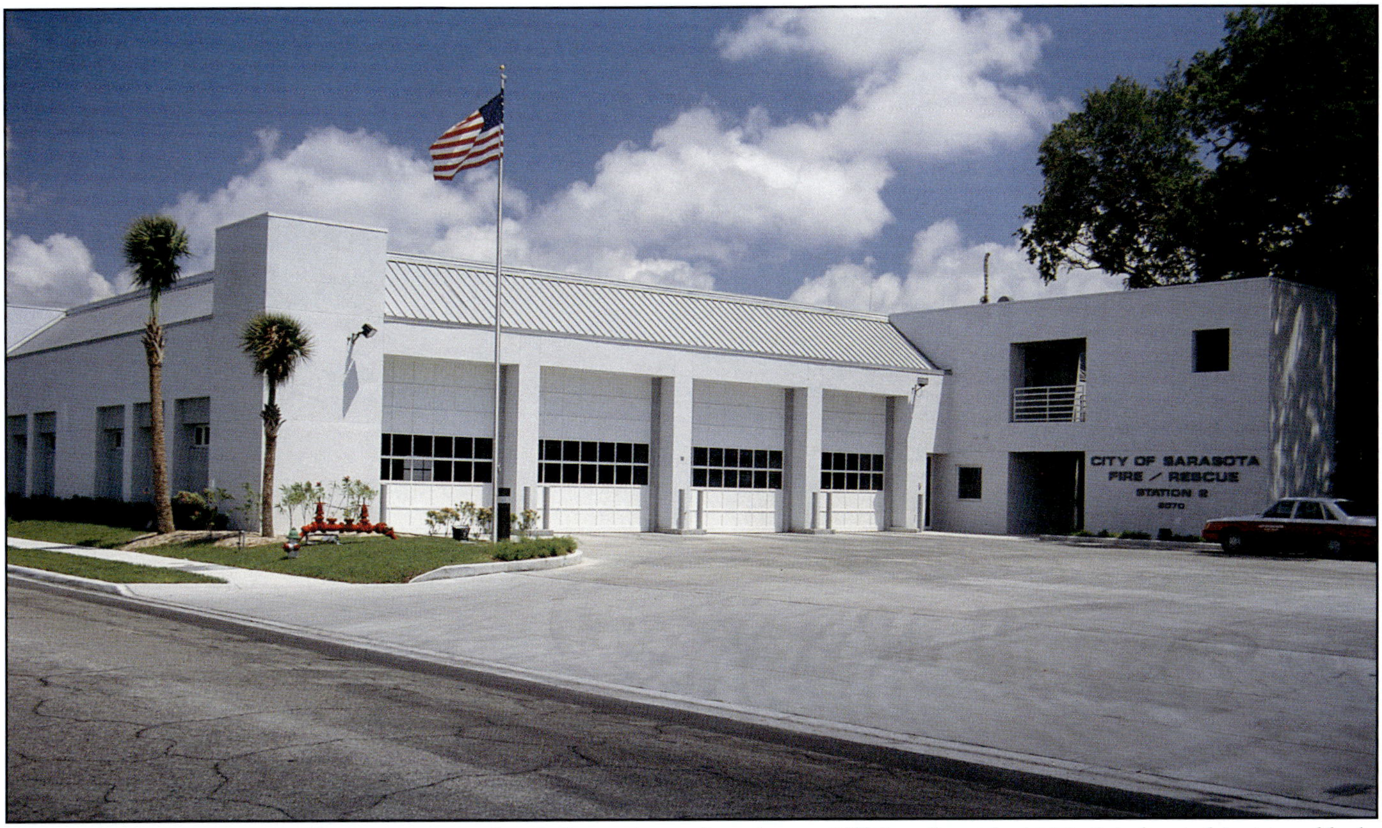

COURTESY SARASOTA FIRE-RESCUE

Fire station #2 at 2070 Waldemere Street replaced the antiquated station on Hillview Street in 1988. It is located just two blocks from Sarasota Memorial Hospital.

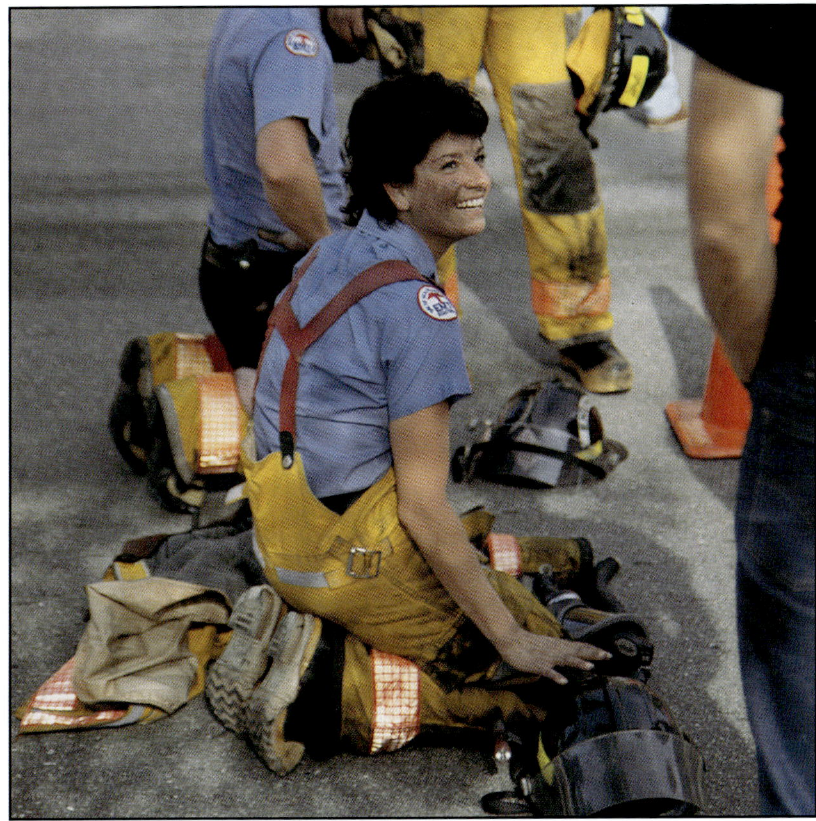

Firefighter Susan Shyne takes a brief rest after firefighting and evacuation operations of Dolphin Towers Condominiums. February, 1992.

COURTESY WAYNE A. WELSH

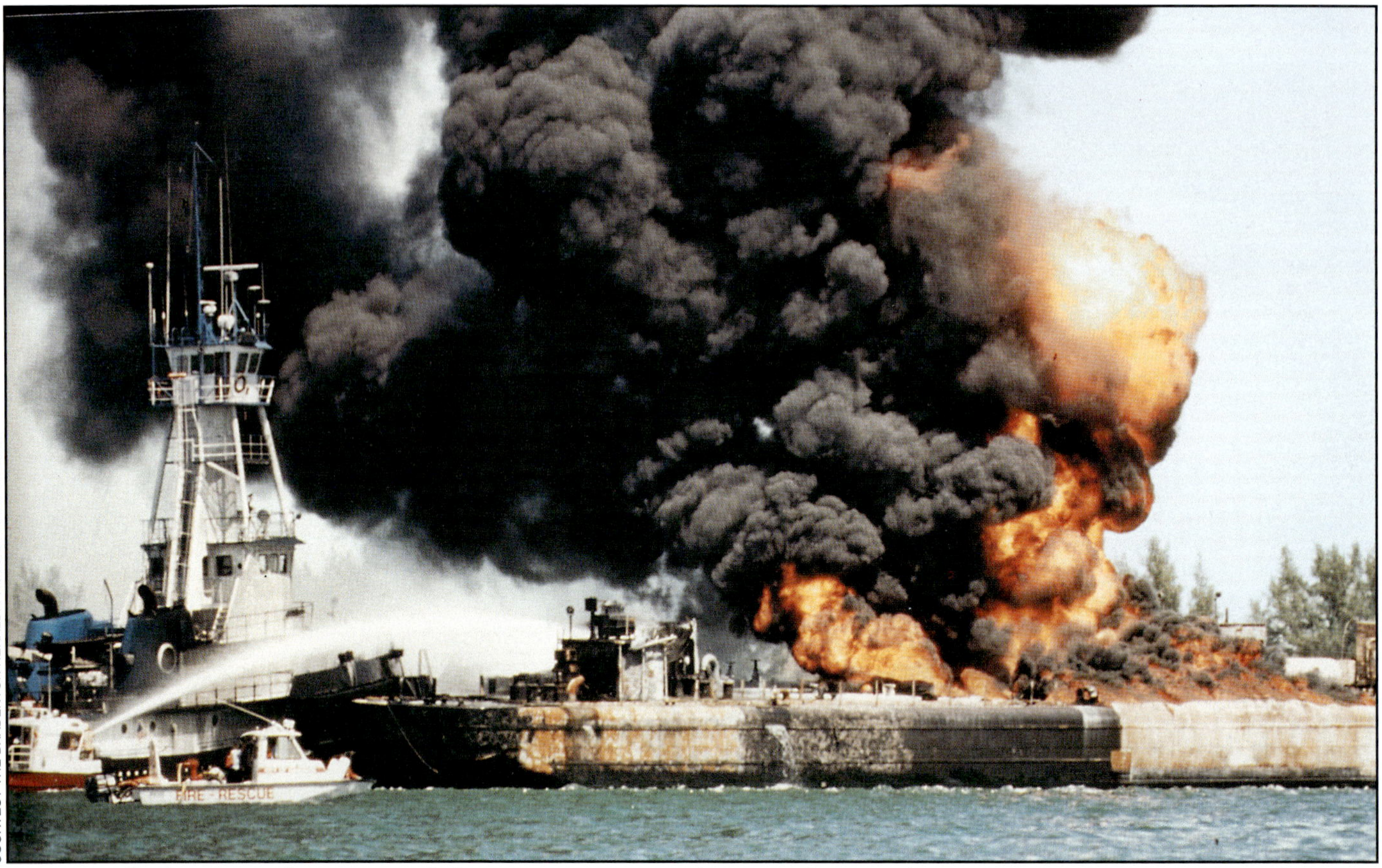

COURTESY THE BRADENTON HERALD. PHOTO BY AL ANDERSON

Sarasota's fire boat, a 25 foot Boston Whaler, prepares to operate its 750 gallon per minute pump. Sarasota was requested to assist neighboring communities after a freighter and two barges collided in Tampa Bay. The fire boat and its crew pumped water for over twelve hours to cool the burning barge which contained 9.4 million gallons of jet fuel. This action helped avoid an ecological disaster by preventing the barge from sinking. The crew at the incident was Battalion Chief Randy Stulce, Captain David Stershic, Mark Tuttle, Gary Potter, and James Jarrett. August 10, 1993.

Modern apparatus are designed for safety and efficiency. Left to right: Truck 13 – Darryl Martin; Special Operations 54 – Lieutenant Keith Austin, Chuck Light; Engine 11 – Tom May, Braille Thomas; R-15 – Mark Tuttle, Greg Loehr (absent due to an emergency response); Battalion 4 – Battalion Chief Thomas Chase. November 12, 1993.

COURTESY WAYNE A. WELSH

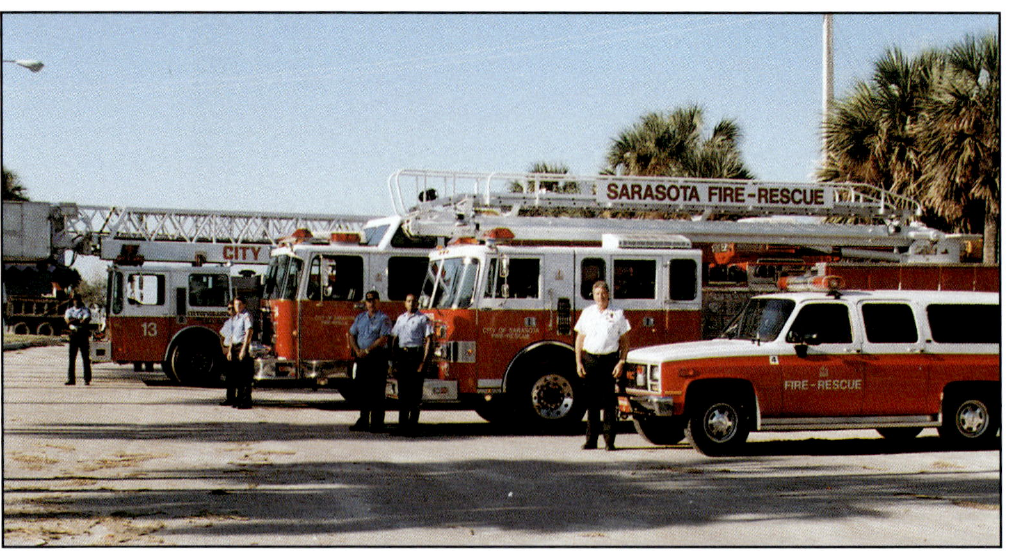

Student's Day in May 1962. Firefighters Hugo Bilter (left) and Thomas Rhoades (right) demonstrate the 1954 Pirsch Aerial to an eager audience.

Nighttime training in front of the Ninth Street Station (later re-numbered to Third Street).

The Plaza Restaurant fire on November 3, 1962 took over two hours to bring under control. Captain A.J. Petellat (left) was one of 30 firemen who battles the blaze.

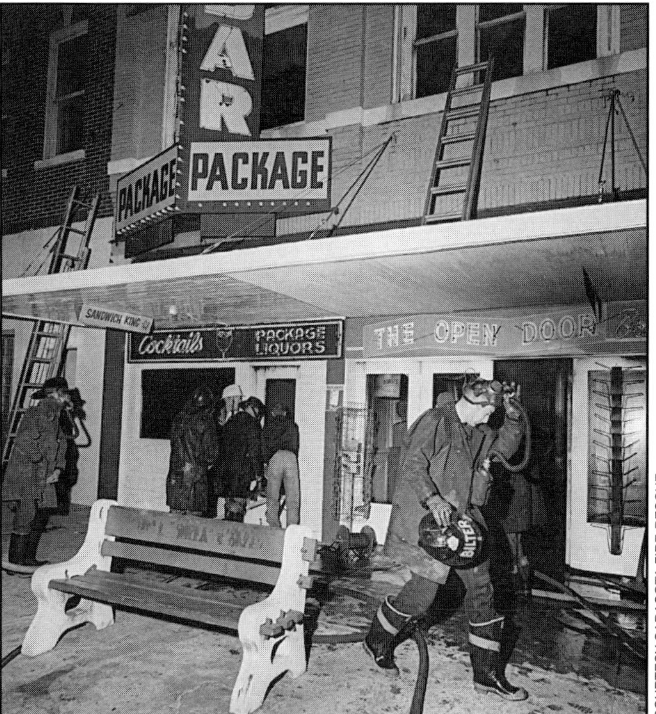

Firefighter Hugo Bilter takes a much needed break.

The 1954 Pirsch Aerial upon delivery to the Sarasota Fire Department. Left to right: Harvey Clemons, A.J. Petellat, Vernon Wallers, Otto Manson, Marion Lawrence, Rufus Fralick, Albert Miller, Dewey Maus, Arthur Drumright, Alfred Lanier, Elmer Taylor, John Stone, Harold Stinchcomb, Bill Wagner, Curtis Tucker, James R. Cowsert, Don Hoover, Maitland Knowles.

Fire department Chaplain, J.D. Hamel (right), assists firefighters extending a hoseline at the Open Door Restaurant Fire. Reverend Hamel has committed himself to caring for the emotional and spiritual needs of Sarasota's firefighters since 1960. His devotion to Sarasota's firefighters has earned him the respect and love of the entire department.

More hose, more water, more help! Firefighting can sometimes be a lonely job as this fireman discovers while stretching the first hoseline at this fully involved wood structure.

CHAPTER 16

BACKDRAFT

Harold R. Stinchcomb was like many young boys who heard the call of the sirens and dreamed of being a fireman or someday a fire chief. His uncle spurred his interest by taking him into the fire stations in Cleveland. Unlike many others, his boyhood dreams became reality when he was appointed the fifth chief of the Sarasota Fire Department on July 12, 1966. Stinchcomb, with only twelve years on the job, replaced retiring Chief Cowsert. Stinchcomb's starting salary was $9300 annually for a 72-hour work week.[1]

One of Stinchcomb's goals was to establish a regional school to train firefighters, which was dedicated June 6, 1971, at 400 North Beneva Road, previously Oriente Avenue. The facility serves a dual purpose. On the north side is a fully functioning fire station. The apparatus floor separates the station from the training academy, located on the south side of the building. Much of the planning was done by William Schultz who along with the other firemen did a great deal of the work themselves.[2,3]

The training academy has the vital function of converting youthful firefighter candidates into safe and knowledgeable firefighters. The academy trains firefighters for Sarasota, Manatee, Desoto, Broward, and Charlotte counties. The academy has even trained candidates from Central America. Academy instructors are seasoned firefighters charged with the responsibility of preparing the candidates for the rigors they will encounter as firefighters. The candidates are exposed to the oppressive heat, choking and blinding smoke, and physical and mental exhaustion that they might experience during a severe fire. The instructors are well aware that this training might someday save the life of one of these future firefighters. Many candidates do not successfully complete the intensive training and seek alternative careers. Those with the resolve to complete the academy training, however, can move on to a challenging and exhilarating career.

A four-story smoke tower enhances the realism of the training. The tower can be charged with smoke, which requires trainees to accomplish their objectives in total darkness while wearing breathing apparatus. A typical scenario requires a group of six firefighters to advance a hoseline from the ground level up the stairs and extinguish a fire on the fourth floor. The tower also provides a location for training in repelling and rope rescue.

Liquid petroleum gas (LPG) is extremely dangerous when exposed to fire. Firefighter Don Grant places his life and a hoseline between an engine fire and an LPG tank. Grant managed to cool the tank and prevent its explosion. December 19, 1974.

COURTESY SARASOTA FIRE-RESCUE

All previous candidates recall the physical fitness training and running laps around the training academy track. A spring-fed lake provides an ideal location for learning to draft water from existing water sources such as lakes, canals, pools, and the bay. The procedure is used to fight fires when hydrants are not available. The lake also provides a location to test the pumping abilities of fire apparatus.

Two highlights at the academy are the pit fires and liquid petroleum gas fires. Firefighter candidates must accomplish a mock rescue through a thirty-foot high wall of flame located in a pit of intensely burning flammable liquid. Firefighters use hosestreams to create a corridor in the one hundred feet long wall of flames. The rescue of an injured victim is simulated when a fellow firefighter is carried through the opening while the candidates hold back the flames using the hose streams.

Firefighters must also stabilize a burning cylinder of liquid petroleum gas and close a leaking valve under heavy fire conditions. Firefighters operate under the protection of hoselines in this particularly dangerous encounter. This same situation has claimed countless lives throughout the country because of the likelihood of the cylinder to explode. At the academy the same learning experience is recreated without the risk of explosion, although, all firefighting operations have inherent dangers, even during training. The quality of the training program is largely responsible for the department's excellent safety record. The department has not had a firefighter killed in the line of duty, a record they hope to continue.

The service division of the Sarasota Fire Department has shared a common parcel of land with the training academy. The department's highly skilled mechanics have specialized in the repair and maintenance of fire apparatus. They have had the equipment and knowledge to repair apparatus as diverse as fireboats, fire engines, aerial platforms, and rescue units.

Firefighting places tremendous wear on apparatus, engines, and pumps. They run for long hours, under the worst of conditions, and without time to warm up gradually. The mechanics have done a commendable job in keeping the department's fleet of apparatus in first-class operating condition. They are well aware that every time an engine responds, both the citizens' and the firefighters' lives depend on the quality of their work.

The dangers of firefighting had become apparent to Stinchcomb when he responded to a fire at the Ritz Theatre before he became chief. Stinchcomb was scheduled to leave for vacation just thirty minutes after the alarm was received. The theatre manager had attempted to extinguish the fire using a carbon tetrachloride fire extinguisher. Stinchcomb became exposed to phosgene gas, a poisonous byproduct of carbon tetrachloride fire extinguishers. As a result, the young fire lieutenant spent ten days in the hospital and six weeks away from work while recuperating.[4]

One of the most challenging fires faced by the department during Stinchcomb's tenure was the Liggett Drug Store Fire in 1979. The Liggett Drug Store was located at 1400 Main Street, at the southeast corner of Five Points. The building was once known as the Sarasota Bank and was owned by Jim Olson at the time of the fire.[5,6]

A backdraft explosion at the Liggett Drug Store Fire resulted in the narrow escape of five firefighters. Fifty-one firefighters and twenty pieces of apparatus fought the April 1, 1979 blaze. The Liggett Drug Store building once served as the landmark Bank of Sarasota.

The fire was believed to have started by a malfunction in an ice maker control box. It burned upward inside a wood partition wall and grew for several hours in a confined four-foot space created by a drop ceiling. This confined space had been created because the building had been extensively remodeled. The fire continued to burn in the confined space while using up all the available oxygen. The result was an atmosphere of superheated gases that were extremely flammable but starved for oxygen. The fire sat waiting for a fresh supply of oxygen.[7] The fire department received the alarm while firefighters were checking their apparatus for the day and were preparing for their traditional Sunday brunch. The owner Jim Olson was visiting a friend on the east side of town.[8]

The department received the call at 9:04 a.m. The first units to arrive encountered a large, two-story brick and block building with wood frame interior. They saw smoke inside the structure seeping out around the upper doorways and roof. The doors were forced opened. The initial attack crew consisted of Vince Hernandez, Willis Bell, and Terry Howells on one hoseline and Lieutenant Rod Cameron and James Frazier on a second hoseline. The crew entered the building from the door at Five Points. The firefighters penetrated into the building, crawling on their hands and knees with hoseline in hand. They could hear the crackling of the fire and the popping sound of exploding aerosol cans. A low rumbling noise came from the rear of the building followed instantaneously by a loss of visibility and tremendous heat buildup. Lieutenant Cameron issued the order to back out, and the firefighters instinctively began to retreat, abandoning the hoselines.[9]

Within seconds the rumbling became deafening, the ceiling tiles luminous, and the heat unbearable. Before the firefighters could exit, a tremendous internal explosion, known as a backdraft, took place that rocked the building. Four firefighters were bodily propelled through the air a distance of fifteen feet onto the asphalt outside. The nozzleman, firefighter Vince Hernandez, remained inside. Hernandez battled the intense heat and lack of visibility as he scrambled towards the exit. His comrades were elated to see him emerge through the heavy stream of smoke. Windows were blown out sending shards of glass one-hundred feet in all directions. Four of the five firefighters on the initial attack lines suffered injuries. Flames had enveloped the entire ground floor immediately following their narrow escape.[10]

Fred Soto, Sr., the former mayor of Sarasota, became aware of the fire and telephoned his friend and building owner, Jim Olson. He proceeded to relay the story of the grave situation. Jim immediately jumped into his car and rushed across town toward the scene of the fire.[11]

Approximately half way to the drugstore Olson realized that the date was April 1: April Fool's Day. Stubborn and unwilling to give his friend the satisfaction of what he considered a masterfully performed April Fool's Day prank, Olson turned his car around and headed for home. He chuckled to himself until he was almost home. Finally, his humor turned to uncertainty. What if his friend was telling the truth? He again turned his car around and went directly to the drug store.[12]

COURTESY SARASOTA HERALD TRIBUNE

Chief Harold Stinchcomb directs firefighting operations at the Liggett Drug Store fire. Over 3000 gallons of water per minute were used to control the fire.

Olson arrived to see a great plume of black smoke rising skyward. Apparatus and hoselines surrounded his building. Three thousand gallons of water per minute were being pumped into the structure and onto adjacent buildings through aerial and ground nozzles. The original goal of saving the drugstore had shifted to preventing the fire from spreading to the adjacent art gallery and down Main Street. Even though the drug store was a total loss, the blaze was extinguished without damaging adjacent businesses.[13]

Fifty-one fire fighters staffing twenty pieces of apparatus battled the blaze for more than four hours.

Eight firefighters suffered injuries from the fire and to this day Jim Olson thinks twice before considering anything as just an April Fool's Day joke.[14]

Even before the Liggett Drug Store Fire, Chief Stinchcomb made great strides towards the goal of making Sarasota a community safe from the threat of fire. He believed in a proactive approach, in which efforts are directed towards preventing fires from starting, rather than a reactive approach. In a reactive approach efforts are devoted towards rapidly extinguishing fires after they have started. Departments that believe in reactive firefighting without adequate fire prevention have turned many buildings into parking lots that remain as monuments to their failures. Sarasota Fire Department's fire prevention program concentrated on several areas: public education, company fire inspection, plans review, and code enforcement.

The department has taken advantage of every opportunity to bring the fire safety message to the public.

Firefighters have spoken to schools, churches, and civic groups. Children seem to best remember the grand tours of the fire station. For a young child to ring a bell, blow a siren, sit in a fire engine, and wear a real fire helmet has been a dream come true for thousands of Sarasota's children. Firefighters have hoped that these children would share their knowledge of fire safety with their parents and grow up to be firesafe adults themselves.

Halton Building Fire on April 6, 1976 destroyed the two-story historic structure at 41 Pineapple Avenue south near Five Points.

In addition to educational programs, firefighters have visited commercial businesses annually and performed company fire inspections. The inspections assist local businesses by identifying practices and conditions that could potentially start a fire. The inspections also afford the firefighters the opportunity to become familiar with the building and its contents under non-threatening conditions. This familiarity has proven invaluable to firefighters when they are called upon to function in blinding smoke and intense heat.

The fire prevention division was responsible for reviewing all plans for commercial construction and remodeling. Its purpose was to ensure that the designs comply with all appropriate fire and life safety codes. This practice ensures the safety of the employees, customers, firefighters, contents, and the structure itself. Problems found are corrected on the drawing board, avoiding costly modifications during construction or future loss of life.

The department took an innovative approach to

Firefighter Pete Robins teaches local children about fire safety during a Fire Prevention Day tour.

The Sarasota Fire Department in 1976. This photo was taken from the roof of the Van Wezel Performing Arts Center.

providing fire protection in large structures. Builders were made to share the responsibility by designing fire alarms, sprinklers, and standpipes, depending on the height and square footage of the structure, into their buildings. Designing fire protection into the structure allowed the fire department to provide adequate life safety yet remain modest in size. These fire protection codes were implemented locally while still being discussed nationally. Sarasota's codes were among the first in the state and were used as models throughout the United States.

The fire department is an organization with a rich

Sarasota's first female firefighter, Charlena Jenkins, demonstrates a carry using a fellow academy student Jim Bon Ami.

and proud tradition. Firefighters have guarded that tradition jealously and have always resisted change. Firefighters have always felt that they were members of an exclusive fraternity. The department lagged years behind the federal government's lead concerning civil rights and other social issues. Sarasota's first Afro-American firefighter was hired in 1975. Saul Johnson joined the department 21 years after Brown verses Board of Education — the Supreme Court epic desegregation decision.

The mental image of the rugged, masculine firefighter took a back seat in 1987 when the department hired its first female firefighter, Charlena Jenkins. Jenkins became the first of five female fire fighters who successfully completed the academy training that year to become career firefighters with the Sarasota Fire Department. Of course, certain small changes did occur within the department: firemen became firefighters, manpower became personnel, and minor alterations were made to the living facilities. Otherwise, the department conducted business as usual.[15]

The department introduced the community to its newest fire station at 2070 Waldemere Street. The new station replaced the antiquated Station #2 on Hillview Street in 1988. The department set an example for the business community by installing sprinklers, standpipes, and a complete fire alarm system. The two-story structure cost $1,000,000 and is centrally located between three hospitals, dozens of nursing homes, and a multitude of doctors' offices and residences.[16] Chief Harold R. Stinchcomb formally retired December 28, 1988. He devoted nearly 35 years to the department, serving for more than 22 years as fire chief. In his letter announcing his retirement, Stinchcomb wrote, "I am proud of the fact that this city has been in a leadership role by providing modern fire codes and ordinances. These codes and ordinances make the city of Sarasota one of the safest places to be if you are unfortunate enough to have a fire or medical emergency. I'm extremely proud of our fire department and the personnel that make it one of the best departments in the country." Stinchcomb's replacement Thomas Fields, said that, "Stinchcomb took a good fire department and made it a truly professional fire department."[17,18]

Chapter 17

From a Distance: Communications in the Fire Department

As the Bay View House burned and the smoke and ash were chased skyward by the flame, the town clamored with anxiety. The fire crackled and popped and parts of the roof and walls came crashing down. The commotion was deafening and the moment so intense that the booming voice of Henry Behrens was likened to a horn heard through the fog. His voice somehow added direction to what otherwise would have been chaos. Thus were the makings of the first communications used by the Sarasota Fire Department.

Early communications used by the department were so simple they made sense. Orders were given face to face. One could easily tell when someone heard the message and understood. Likewise, one could see confusion and fear in a person's eyes when it existed. When the officer and firefighter were separated by a distance, he simply shouted. As distances increased, he shouted even louder. Behrens had little trouble directing firefighting efforts this way because the distances spanned by the early bucket brigades were short. When hose carts and fire engines made their debut in Sarasota, the fire laddies found themselves spread over distances of hundreds and sometimes thousands of feet. The need arose to convey information over distances too great to shout. "charge the line, we need more pressure, send for help," and "call the chief" were all typical early messages.[1]

The fire department began using simple semaphore signals to span these great distances. A fireman would wave his hat or helmet in a specific fashion to another fireman at a great distance. Members were required to know each of ten different messages. Nighttime communications was similar except that a lantern was used instead of a hat.[2]

Fire alarms were just as primitive. Most fires occurred at night and the town had to be awakened from a sound sleep. Shouts of "FIRE" and pistol shots seemed as familiar a sound as the mullet jumping in the bay. Instinctively the volunteers would leap into action and report to the station. The firefighting equipment was promptly pulled through the moonlit streets to the scene of the fire. After pulling the hose carts, chemical engines, and ladder wagon to the scene, the volunteers began the arduous job of firefighting.[3]

A special meeting was called by Mayor A.B. Edwards July 1, 1915 to discuss installing a fire alarm system. The system was approved and installed immediately. A citizen reporting a fire would contact the operator by telephone. The operator in turn would immediately report the alarm over telephone line number 5000. This rang the phone lines into the ice and power plant, fire station, city council chambers, and pumping station. Someone at the ice and power plant would then blow the fire whistle at the plant that would signal the volunteers to report to the fire station. The operator remained on the line until she received a telephoned response from the fire station. Instructions for fire reporting were printed and pasted on the front cover of each telephone directory in the city. The newly installed fire whistle was tested daily at noon. On its maiden test the whistle seriously frightened many of the locals who were not yet aware of the new installation. This fire

TELEPHONE 249

Sarasota Fire Department

OFFICE OF THE CHIEF
HENRY BEHRENS
Sarasota, - Florida

Sarasota, Fla.,7/28/15

-:NOTICE :-

-: TO MEMBERS OF SARASOTA FIRE DEPARTMENT :-
All signals to be given facing the truck squarly, these are "Semophore"
signals, to be given with the helmet.
Day Signals.
#I - Ready for water,- Swing hat across legs at the knee viz:-
----

#2 - water in #I Line,- Swing hat right side of body,from knee to
level of right shoulder, viz:-------------------.-----

#3 - Water in #2 Line,- Swing hat right side of body, from knee to
perpendicular over head, viz:----------------

#4 - Water in #3 Line,- Swing hat left side of body, from knee to
level of left shoulder, viz:--------------

#5 - High pressure,- Swing hat with right hand over head, back and
forth, viz:------------------------------------

#6 - Water shut-off,- Swing hat with right hand in Horizontal Circle,
viz:----------------------------

#7 - Complete shut down,- Swing hat with left hand from level of
shoulder to perpendicular over head,
viz:--------------------

#8 - Take up hose,- Swing hat with right hand in vertical, on right
side of body with full arm swing,viz:-------   *Circle*

#9 - Calling the Chief,- Swing hat with right hand, shoulder hight
horizontally across body, viz:---------------

#IO- Trouble,- Swing hat in large circles from knee over head, viz:-

- - - - - - - - -

This order to take effect this day, JULY,28, 1915.
(P. S.) Night Signals are the same, except that a Lantern is used.)
(Signed

Henry Behrens

Chief Fire Department,

City of Sarasota, Fla.

The Gamewell fire alarm box system was dependent on a loop of interconnecting wires. These wires were frequently damaged by storms and tree limbs. Captain Maus performs a routine test.

alarm system had one critical shortcoming. The citizen had to have access to a phone. Behrens updated the system by replacing the whistle with a large electric siren mounted on a tower in back of the fire station. The siren was audible over the entire city and beyond.[4,5,6,7,8]

Chief Knowles was acutely aware of how rapidly fires grew once they started. He also knew that prompt notification of the fire department was essential for keeping the fire menace in check. Wasting those first precious minutes could have grave consequences. Knowles presented his case before the city council and was granted funds to install a new fire alarm system similar to those used in the "big cities".

The Gamewell Company of Newton, Massachusetts supplied the necessary equipment, and the fire department supplied the sweat labor for the new system. Sarasotans began to see the unmistakable red fire alarm boxes appear in 1925. Twenty-three boxes were strategically placed throughout the city and were mounted on pre-existing telephone and electrical poles.[9,10]

The boxes were originally organized on three circuits looped together by insulated copper wire. Twenty

The Gamewell Fire Alarm System allowed the department to receive prompt notification of fires beginning in 1925. To the right of the Gamewell System is Chief James R. Cowsert.

miles of the wire were strung overhead, which created the three loops of fire alarm boxes that originally protected the city. Eventually, over thirty-one miles of cable and 73 boxes were installed.[11,12]

Each fire alarm box was numbered. Firemen were expected to know the number of each box and their location. When an alarm box was pulled by a citizen, the number of the box would ring on the gong at the fire station, thus indicating the area of the alarm. If Box No. 15 was pulled, for example, the gong would sound one time, pause, and sound another five times indicating Box No. 15. The entire message would repeat two or more times. Instantly the firemen would know the alarm was coming from the box located on the northeast corner of Main Street and Lemon Avenue, across from the Seaboard Airline Railroad Depot. The gong, which was actually a large brass bell with a striking mechanism, hung handsomely in the fire station. A visual indicator would display the numerical value of the box and a punch register would record the numbers on a tape, thus making a permanent record.[13,14]

An integral part of the Gamewell system was the fire horn. It was installed outside the Arcade Building and sounded whenever a box was pulled. "The first time it blew, the people at the Sarasota Hotel thought the animals at the circus had escaped," claimed Chief Cowsert. "We called a farmer on the edge of town to find out if he could hear it. He told us to wait until a cow stopped bellowing and he would try to hear it. The `bellowing' was the horn," Cowsert added. The purpose of the horn was to notify off-duty firemen of an emergency so they may respond.[15,16]

When the fire department moved to the Third Street Station and later to Fourth Street, the Gamewell system and fire horn moved with it. Although the Gamewell system remained in use, the fire horn was removed in December 1955.[17,18]

The advent of the frequency modulation (FM) radio was a boon to fire department communications. Prior to the FM radio, firemen would lose communication with the station as soon as their apparatus responded to a fire. When firemen required additional assistance, they summoned help using the closest telephone or the telegraph in any of the gamewell fire alarm boxes. FM radios allowed communication with the station to request additional assistance, to provide the correct location of a fire, and to give the estimated time required to bring a blaze under control. Apparatus could be dispatched to additional fires as soon as they had extinguished a blaze rather than after they returned to the station.[19]

Mobile radios installed in fire apparatus provided a vital link between firefighters on-scene and those at the station. Ralph Parsons performs a radio test.

The first FM radio was installed in the fire chief's car during the time when Knowles was the fire chief. Both the police and fire departments originally shared the same frequency. Firemen took turns monitoring the General Electric FM transmitter located at the fire station. Sarasota's first portable FM radio was the size of a suitcase. The portable FM radio allowed the firefighters freedom to move about on the fire ground.

Early in his administration Chief Stinchcomb installed a cord-type PBX telephone switchboard at the Fourth Street Fire Station. This eliminated the old system of having the "fire-phone" ring in all of the fire stations each time the fire department emergency phone number was called by the public, which previously disrupted the fire fighters' daily work routines. Each day a schedule was posted that assigned four hour periods of "watch duty" at the switchboard and radio. This was the forerunner of a communications center for the department.[20,21]

Chief Stinchcomb was a licensed ham radio opera-

Prior to CommCe, dispatching was done from this General Electric Base Station radio. Firefighters took turns staffing the G.E. radio and PBX switchboard. Left to right: James Johnston, Clarence Addy.

tor and for many years, was responsible himself for the maintenance of the old Gamewell fire alarm box system. The Gamewell system with its outside, exposed wires could be easily disabled if a tree fell and damaged any portion of the wire. Stinchcomb was well aware of the benefits that a radio-operated fire alarm box system would have: citizen initiated fire alarms could be transmitted by radio waves, each box worked independently, and other boxes would continue working if one box was damaged.[22,23]

The Gamewell system still contained the original boxes, which were purchased in 1925, and many boxes of mixed vintage that had been added through the years. The entire system was obsolete. In order to maintain insurance rating credit from the fire underwriters, it needed to be replaced.[24,25]

In a great step forward in 1970, the department purchased 80 radio boxes and monitoring equipment from Eagle-Picher Industries of Inglewood, California. At the same time the department began constructing a new communications center to handle the department's dispatching needs, which would be operated by specially trained civilian fire dispatchers.[26,27]

"CommCe," as the new center was called, was con-

structed at the east end of the central fire station on Fourth Street in an area previously used for hose drying and storage. It was equipped with a telephone switchboard, fire alarm box monitoring equipment, and the department's two-way radio system, all of which were built into new console cabinetry. The radio telemetry system used radio waves instead of interconnecting wires. Becoming operational on February 26, 1971, it was the first such system in Florida and the third radio telemetry system to be rated nationally.[28,29]

At about that time, CommCe began operations with only one communications controller on duty at a time. Under the direction of Lieutenant Elbert E. Friend, the four dispatchers ran the nerve center of the fire department. Upon taking a request for emergency assistance, they evaluated the reported incident and decided the type and quantity of equipment to dispatch. Alone most of the time, the communication controllers made many decisions based on their own knowledge and instincts. Remaining level-headed has always been a

Radio-transmitted fire alarm boxes replaced the Gamewell System in February 1971. Lieutenant Albert Miller tests a box on Siesta Drive, east of Tamiami Trail South.

Communications controller Bill Parker monitors radio traffic. Prior to computers, communications controllers relied on maps, charts, address tubs, and memory.

COURTESY SARASOTA FIRE-RESCUE

chief concern, but as Lieutenant Friend said, "What is an emergency to the person on the street is our everyday business." Some calls received on the emergency telephone lines have been as tense as, "my house is on fire and my baby is trapped inside." Others simply have required the dispatching of an engine to an alarm received from one of the many fire alarm boxes located in the city. CommCe dispatched over 500 calls of all types in its first year of operation.[30,31]

CommCe entered the space age when the department installed a new quarter million dollar dispatch system in 1978. The new computer did not replace the competent communications controllers but improved their efficiency by assisting them with making split-second decisions. Under the old system, the controllers, who sit surrounded by maps, charts, and street address listings hunted for the incident location in an indexed tub of addresses. They also determined which apparatus were available, which station was closest, and which types of apparatus were required to handle the emergency. The new system eliminated most of these decisions. Every street in Sarasota city and county has been entered into the computer. Specific information on the number and type of apparatus needed and station response areas are preplanned and programmed into the computer. When the emergency call is received, the communication controller enters the address in the computer. The terminal instantly displays which apparatus are available, the type of structure involved, the nearest hydrants, and which apparatus to send on a first, second, or third alarm. The push of a button sends the information to a printer at the appropriate station at the same time as the controller broadcasts the information by radio. In this manner, the computerized system has drastically reduced the time required to dispatch emergency calls.[32,33]

CommCe extended its dispatch services in 1984 to the Fruitville and Northeast Fire Districts. This expansion resulted from the merger of those districts with the South Trail District to form the Metropolitan Sarasota Fire-Rescue District currently known as the Sarasota County Fire Department. CommCe had been contracting dispatch services to the South Trail District since 1978.[34,35]

Sarasota citizens again reaped the benefits of technology on September 17, 1985 when the county-wide enhanced 9-1-1 system materialized. Citizens could receive the appropriate type of emergency response by dialing 9-1-1 on any telephone, regardless of whether they needed fire, medical, or police assistance. All 9-1-1 calls are received at the 9-1-1 center located in the Sarasota County Administration Building. The calls received are rapidly transferred to the appropriate agency for dispatching. The 9-1-1 system eliminated the need for different emergency phone numbers for different agencies and districts.[36]

The enhanced 9-1-1 system automatically displays the exact location of the phone being used to report an emergency. Callers who have become unconscious or have been so panicked that they hang up before giving their address have had their lives saved by the enhanced 9-1-1 system's technology. In 1992 CommCe dispatched a total of 21,636 emergency calls, the majority of which were received through 9-1-1. 9,405 of those calls were for the city of Sarasota.[37]

Diligent efforts on the part of communication controllers and firefighters place apparatus and personnel at the scene of an emergency in the city of Sarasota in less than four minutes from the time of the initial call. Even so, some patients' condition can be so grave that they die during those first precious minutes. During the 1980's the department searched for ways to cut down the time required to get help to the patient. Driving faster was certainly not an acceptable solution since it would compromise citizens' safety for a savings of only a few seconds. The department found its answer with Emergency Medical Dispatch (EMD).[38]

EMD turns family members and bystanders into rescuers. Trained communications controllers provide step-by-step instruction to the caller over the phone. The caller is then able to provide first aid for such emergencies as choking, bleeding, seizures, childbirth, and drowning based on physician-approved protocols read by the controller. The controller's calm and reassuring voice, combined with easy to follow instructions, turns frantic callers into the first rescuers on the scene.

The effectiveness of EMD was proven when a mother momentarily left her young daughter near the poolside unattended. When she returned, she was horrified to find her child floating lifeless in the pool. Instinctively, she pulled the child from the water and immediately called 9-1-1.

Elbert Friend was appointed the first communications officer on November 1, 1970. He was placed in command of CommCe when it opened in February 1971.

Within seconds the mother was speaking with a communications controller of the Sarasota Fire Department, who assured her that an ambulance was on the way. The mother wept because she saw that the child had stopped breathing and was an ominous dusky blue color.

The mother, not having been trained in CPR, vividly remembers the controller calmly saying, "Listen closely and I will tell you what to do." The mother listened intently and began a series of alternating breaths and chest compressions. Immediate cardiopulmonary resuscitation (C.P.R.) bridged the distance between life and death for the child. Her breaths of life froze the biological clock that otherwise would have ticked away the chance of her daughter's survival.

Tears of joy filled the mother's eyes when the child began to cough. The sound of her daughter's weak attempts to cry were gradually overwhelmed by the approaching siren. A flurry of commotion soon replaced the loneliness that she had felt. Paramedics feverishly worked to stabilize the critically ill child.

Several days in the hospital followed before the child was well enough to be released. Days later the child held a teddy bear given to her by one of the paramedics. It bore the inscription, "Helping Kids Bear It — City of Sarasota Fire-Rescue."

CHAPTER 18

A SECOND CHANCE: EMERGENCY MEDICAL SERVICES

Sarasota's early settlers had a difficult life. It was through their back-breaking labor that most of them earned their living. They used hand tools to cut trees to clear their homesites and to obtain lumber to build their homes. They hunted and fished to feed their families. Life was simple but hard. Injuries and illness took their toll, posing a serious threat to survival.

Early settlers were subject to assault by bobcats, cougars, wolves, alligators, and rattlesnakes. Perhaps the worst bite, however, came from the mosquito. Mosquitoes were not only a nuisance but a serious threat to health because they carried malaria and yellow fever.

Many early settlers suffered from the chills and fever of malaria. New settlers brought illnesses such as tuberculosis since many sick settlers migrated to Florida in hopes that the sub-tropical climate would cure their ailments or at least shorten their recovery.[1]

Individuals frequently suffered the byproduct of their toils in the form of injuries also. Sprains, strains, and lacerations were considered part of everyday life and were frequently ignored. More serious injuries resulted from horse falls, hunting accidents, animal attacks, land clearing, and construction. As Sarasota grew and modernized, train accidents, car wrecks, and

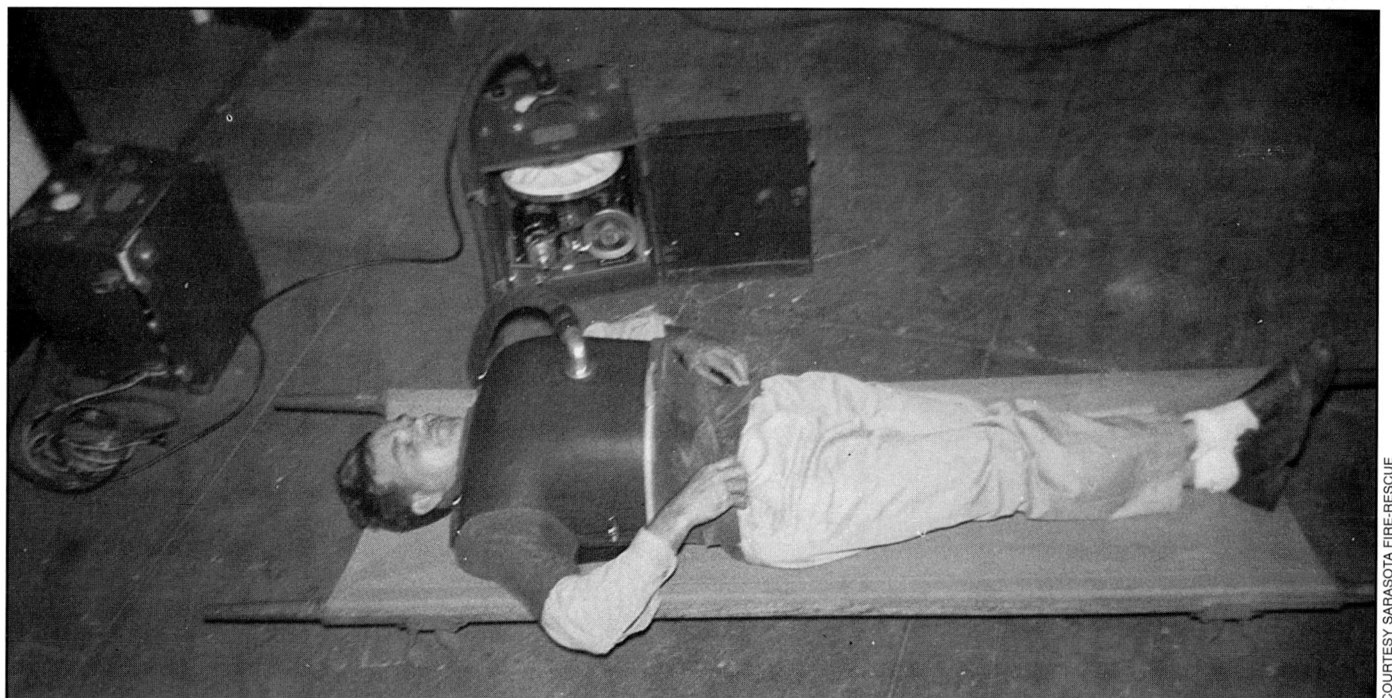

A Mulligan iron lung was purchased in 1944. It was used to resuscitate patients who were unable to breathe on their own such as polio or drowning victims.

the ravages of fire added to the threat.

In a town as small as Sarasota, everyone felt obliged to help when someone was in need. If someone became sick or injured at home, the doctor would be summoned by a family member, friend, or neighbor. House calls were common and the physician was generally a friend of the family. Sometimes the patient would be loaded into a wagon and taken to the doctor's office, which was frequently at the doctor's home. The bumpy wagon ride did little to alleviate the pain or suffering of the patient. Medical "practice" was indeed the best way to describe the early art of medicine, since medical knowledge was still in its infancy, and equipment was rudimentary at best.

The early Sarasota Fire Department was just that — a fire department. It provided fire protection and was neither trained nor equipped to care for the sick or injured. During the 1920's firemen began to receive training in first aid from the American Red Cross. Firemen learned basic bandaging, how to splint an injured limb, how to treat for shock, and other basic skills. Eventually, most of the department were trained in first aid and several firemen became instructors.[2]

The department supplemented their medical armament in 1944 with the purchase of a portable Mulligan iron lung. The iron lung was adaptable for patients from the smallest baby to a person weighing 300 pounds. The lung operated either from storage battery or city electricity. The lung's $1,600 purchase price was unanimously supported by the City and County Commissions, both of which contributed towards its procurement. Its purchase demonstrated a commitment to provide for the health needs of the citizens of Sarasota and to place responsibility squarely on the shoulders of the fire department.[3]

The departments response to requests for medical assistance reflected both their limited training and resources. Calls of a medical nature were handled by quickly loading a car with blankets, splints, bandages, a folding stretcher, the iron lung and an E & J brand resuscitator, inhalator, and aspirator. Beginning in 1939, patients whose breathing had ceased were assisted by firemen using the E & J. Oxygen was forced into the patient's lungs through a mask that was held on the

patient's face. The device essentially breathed for patients who were unable to do so for themselves. In addition to assisting the patient's breathing, the device could suction the patient's mouth, thus clearing the airway of foreign matter that might obstruct breathing. The manufacturer's instructions stated, "Do Not Give Up," and the firemen did their best to live up to that motto. The E & J stood over two feet tall and weighed twenty-nine pounds. Its modern-day replacement fits in the palm of one hand and weighs only four pounds.[4]

The E & J brand resuscitator, inhalator, and aspirator was first used by the department in 1939. Harvey Clemons and Al Lanier prepare to train using the E & J.

Cardiopulmonary resuscitation in its current form was not used in Sarasota outside the hospital until 1971. Prior to that, firemen used a form of artificial respiration called the chest pressure-arm lift technique. Using this technique the firemen placed the patient face down, pressed downward on the back to squeeze the air from the chest, and then lifted the arms to expand the chest. In a limited way it succeeded in moving air into and out of the lungs but provided no circulation of the oxygenated blood through the body when the patient's own heart was unable to do so.[5,6,7,8]

Firemen responded whenever they were called and did the best they could to provide for the medical needs of the community. Early firemen felt "extremely inadequate" in providing any substantial care because of their level of knowledge. Firemen treated their patient and then handed the patient over to a private ambulance company, which was no better trained or

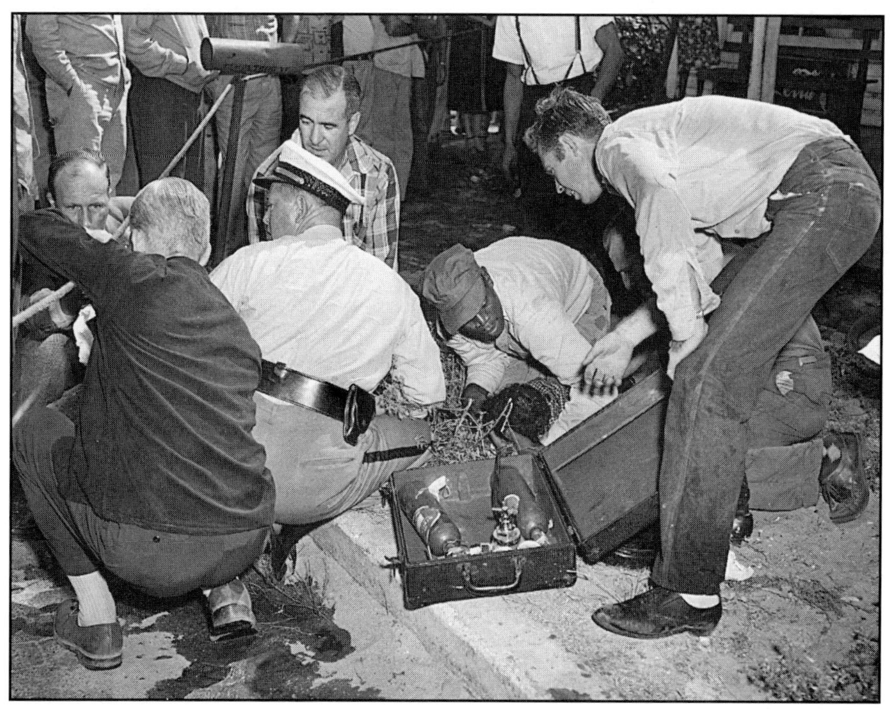

Sarasota firemen and police work together to successfully resuscitate four of five pre-school children trapped in a smokey fire in a downtown residence. The fire was the result of a faulty kerosene stove.

COURTESY THE NEWS, SARASOTA FLORIDA

COURTESY SARASOTA FIRE-RESCUE

Firemen demonstrate the E & J brand resuscitator, inhalator, and aspirator. Vernon Wallers (top left), Curtis W. Tucker (top right), John Stone (middle left), Bill Wagner (middle right), Rufus Fralick (ground).

equipped, but was capable of transporting the patient to the hospital.

Chief Knowles accepted receipt of a retired United States Navy ambulance in 1948 for use as a first aid truck. The reconditioned Dodge was given a fresh coat of paint and pressed immediately into service. Although it was aged, Chief Knowles and the department members considered it a "dream come true." "The fire department has been trying to obtain a well equipped first aid truck for twenty years," according to Chief Knowles. "We have had to load our equipment in a car before answering a call, but now everything will be in this truck and we will be able to answer calls much faster," said Knowles.[9,10]

The first aid truck was equipped with a two-way radio for instant contact with the fire or police station. It also carried the department's combination resuscitator, inhalator, and aspirator, iron lung, first aid supplies, blankets, splints, and some minor firefighting equipment.[11]

The first aid truck and its crew of two responded to and cared for patients with a variety of ailments. Firemen provided first aid, which generally was limited to administering oxygen and neatly splinting or bandaging obvious injuries. Private ambulance companies continued to provide transportation of the patient to the hospital.

Before 1973, most ambulance companies were operated by funeral homes. They sometimes used the

This first aid truck was a retired United States Navy ambulance. It was obtained in 1948.

Private ambulance services transported patients after the fire department provided first aid. The fire department started to provide ambulance services on April 1, 1973.

same vehicle regardless of whether they were transporting an ill patient to the hospital or a deceased person from the morgue to the funeral home. At times, private ambulance companies competed to handle the limited number of calls in order to remain in business. Occasionally, more than one company arrived on scene seeking to transport the same patient and arguments ensued. It has also been rumored that at one vehicle accident involving several patients, one private ambulance crew operated by a funeral home was more anxious to transport the deceased patient than the injured patient.

The private ambulance companies drifted in and out of business like the tide with one exception, Hawkins Funeral Home. Hawkins provided ambulance service to Sarasota beginning in 1961. Hawkins advertised "24 hour service, oxygen equipped ambulances, and attendants trained in first aid." Hawkins grew to a fleet of four air-conditioned and radio-dispatched ambulances. Several of their personnel were eventually trained as emergency medical technicians (EMTs). The fire department and Hawkins maintained that symbiotic relationship for twelve years until it ended abruptly in a storm of political turmoil.[12]

Robert C. Hawkins stated that his ambulance service operated at a loss "due to providing service to underprivileged and medically indigent people." He approached the county commission seeking to establish a special ambulance taxing district to subsidize the service Hawkins was providing to the community. He left them with an ultimatum: to provide the requested $36,000 in annual revenue or he would discontinue the service. The commission heard him loud and clear; that evening the Sarasota Fire Department began making arrangements to take over all emergency ambulance transports. The taxpayers approved the ambulance taxing district but the fire department was selected to provide the service.[13,14,15]

Although Chief Stinchcomb stated that, "Mr. Hawkins gives admirable service and has done so for years," he sought to replace him with a "superior quality service heretofore unheard of in Sarasota." He "envisioned the kind of emergency medical care Los Angeles was giving in cooperation with hospitals as portrayed in the weekly television series Emergency." Stinchcomb traveled to Jacksonville, Florida to model the new Sarasota system after the Jacksonville program established five years before. He was accompanied by Dr Linda Schlumbrecht, an emergency room physician, and Dave Kaighin, an administrator from Sarasota Memorial Hospital. Many experts considered

ONE OF A SERIES

Key Life Saving Equipment Is Carried By 'Rescue 12'

SARASOTA—The Rescue Squad of the Sarasota Fire Department is quartered at the Fourth Street Station. Rescue 12, as it is known, is not meant to provide ambulance service, but instead, carries life saving equipment. Two men respond with it on all emergency-rescue calls.

The most used equipment contained in the car, is the resuscitator, used often on heart or asthma patients, and drowning victims. There are also first aid supplies, blankets, and inflatable plastic splints.

For rescue work, there is hydraulic jacking equipment, a portable oxy-acetyline cutting torch, pry bar, and rope.

All but the newest men of the Fire Department, are holders of American Red Cross advancved first aid cards, and several of the men are certified Instructors.

There are regularly scheduled drills on rescue and resuscitation practices, as part of their regular Fire Department training program.

Due to its location near the beaches, and the possibility of being inaccessible from the mainland, the St. Armands Fire Station also has a resuscitator unit, for use in that area.

The same EMERGENCY phone number is used for fire or rescue calls in the City; 958-3474.

Educational articles such as this one were written by firefighters and featured in the Sarasota Herald Tribune in the 1960's.

ART BY CLARENCE ADDY. COURTESY SARASOTA FIRE-RESCUE

the Jacksonville Emergency Medical System the best in the nation.[16,17]

Sarasota Fire Department officially entered the emergency rescue business on April 1, 1973 equipped with one borrowed ambulance and two other vehicles rented from the Ryder Truck Lines of St. Petersburg. They responded from the stations located on St. Armands Key, Hillview Street, and Fourth Street. The four custom rescue units ordered from the Murphy Manufacturing Company of Wilson, North Carolina did not begin to arrive until November. By January 1974, the department operated a total of five rescue units, one from each station.[18]

Vehicles were not the only resource in scarce supply. For several years Emergency Medical Technicians (EMTs) worked in excess of 100 hours per week because they were in such short supply. The EMTs were extensions of the physicians' eyes and hands. They communicated with the emergency room via two-way radios, and the treatment they rendered was directed by the emergency room physician. The department's EMTs had received over 400 hours of instruction, which included lessons in anatomy, heart-lung resuscitation, and defensive driving from the Sarasota

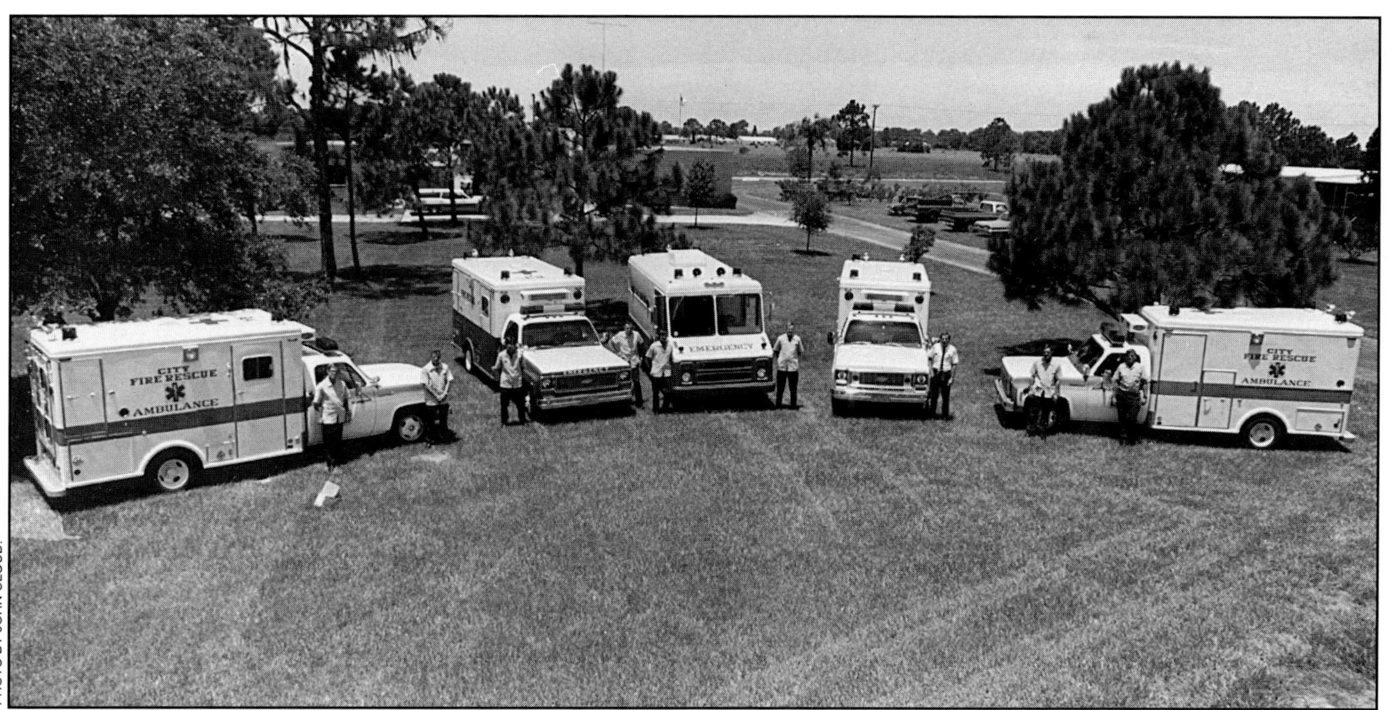

PHOTO BY JOHN CLOUD.

COURTESY SARASOTA JOURNAL

Ambulance fleet of the Sarasota Fire Department in January of 1974.

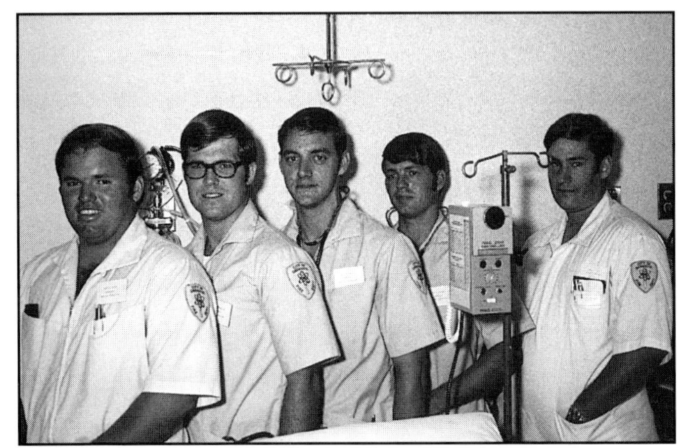

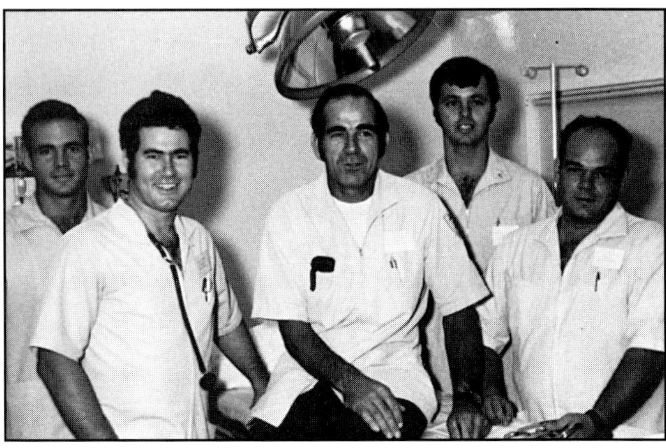

Sarasota's first EMT class graduated in June of 1972 from Sarasota County Vocational Technical Center. The first class had ten members. Photo on left, left to right: Gary Smith, John Gingras Jr., Dale Oswalt, James McKinnon, and Robert Lamb. Photo on right, left to right: Robert Petellat, Daniel Coffman, Vernon Fryer, Robert Bullard, and Donald Grant.

County Vocational Technical Center. They also spent 100 hours at Sarasota Memorial Hospital's emergency room doing hands-on training. This hands-on training provided invaluable interaction with the emergency room physicians and developed a mutual trust which contributed greatly towards the success of the program. The Sarasota EMTs received more than five times the training required by law before the department gave them their stamp of approval. The department's first EMTs graduated on August 18, 1972.[19,20,21]

Doctor Linda Schlumbrecht was the primary advo-cate and defender of the program from the medical community. "There was no packaged course at the time because we were treading new waters," said Schlumbrecht. "The first EMTs were people who weren't afraid to tread the waters with us. There were no standards because we were making the standards as we went. We were all renegades." Because of her devotion and primary role in establishing the rescue service, Schlumbrecht is affectionately known as "The Mother of EMS" in Sarasota.[22,23]

Starting in October of 1973, ten EMTs embarked on

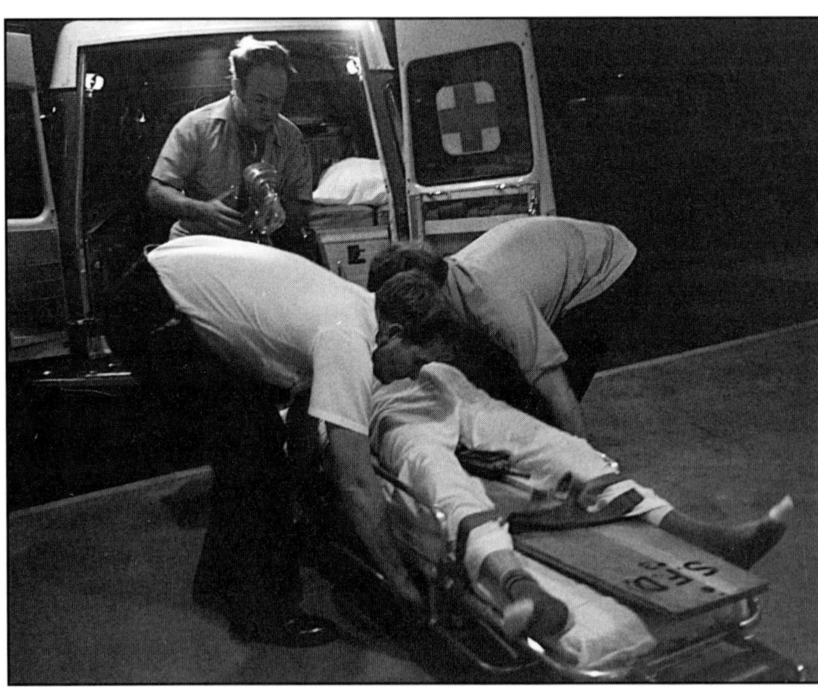

EMT's Keith Hildreth (top) and John Gingras (right) assisted by Battalion Captain Elmer Taylor (left) unload a stroke victim at Sarasota Memorial Hospital.

an additional 500 hours of training that would qualify them to perform advanced life-saving procedures at the scene of an emergency. These new EMT IIs learned to administer medications through intravenous (IV) life-lines. They learned to perform endotracheal intubation by gently placing a tube through patients' vocal cords in order to provide lifesaving breaths and to protect their airways from vomitus. They were also trained to use the department's new heart-lung machines. This device consisted of an oxygen-powered piston that rhythmically compressed the patient's chest and a tube that attached to the patient's airway and alternately provided breaths.[24]

In January 1974 EMT II Don Grant performed the first defibrillation outside of a hospital in Sarasota. Grant found the patient without pulses or breathing and in v-fib. After transmitting an EKG to the hospital, the order to defibrillate was given by Doctor Raymond Stratton. Grant, who had the training, equipment, and courage attempted the new procedure and delivered the patient to the hospital breathing normally and with pulses. The Sarasota Fire Department was the third department in Florida after Jacksonville and Miami to attempt this procedure. Doctor Stratton said that the patient "never would have made it to the hospital were it not for the EMTs quick action."[26]

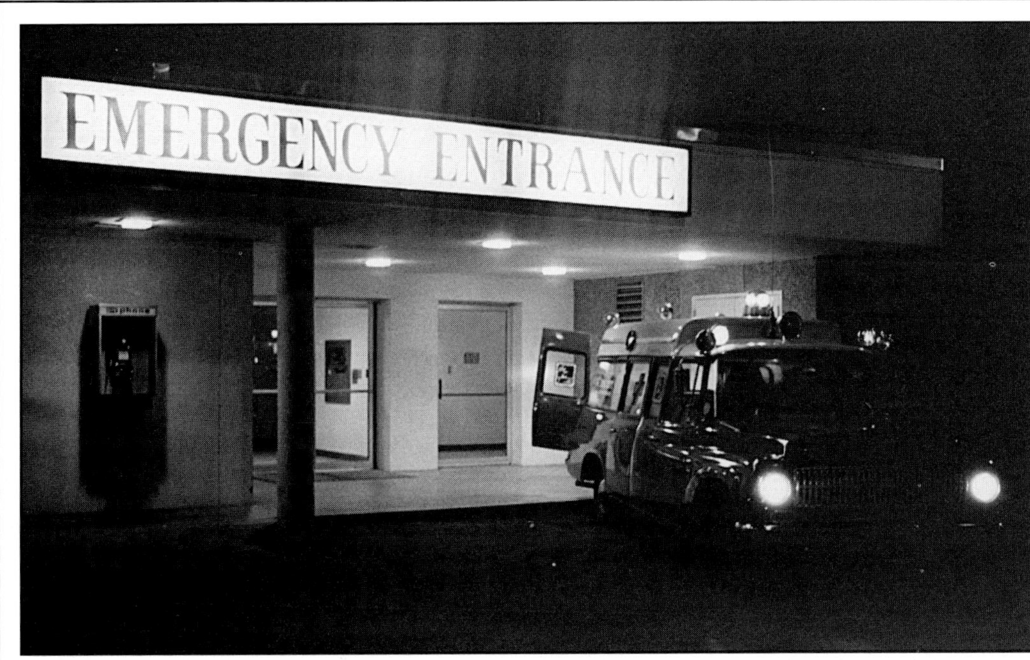

Rescue-2 delivers a patient to the emergency entrance of Sarasota Memorial Hospital.

The use of electrocardiograph telemetry (ET), a byproduct of the space exploration sciences, propelled the rescue program into the future. It allowed the EMT IIs to visualize the heart's electrical activity on a monitor and to transmit simultaneously the information via telemetry radio to the hospital. The emergency room physician specifies the course of treatment via radio. In the event that the heart is in ventricular fibrillation (v-fib), a life-threatening rhythm resulting in a lack of heartbeat, the doctor can order the EMT IIs to defibrillate. Defibrillation passes an electrical current through the heart in much the way jumper cables are used to start a stalled automobile.[25]

In June 1976 the department's EMT IIs traveled to Miami and successfully completed the state's new paramedic exam. Although EMTs still served on the department, the title paramedic was given to those who have received the advanced training. Yet paramedics were received with mixed reviews. The community at large received them with open arms, since a number of citizens were living tributes to the competence of the paramedics. Some physicians, however, felt threatened by the paramedics and felt that they were practicing medicine since paramedics performed many of the procedures previously reserved to physicians. Paramedics, however, functioned under the authority and license of

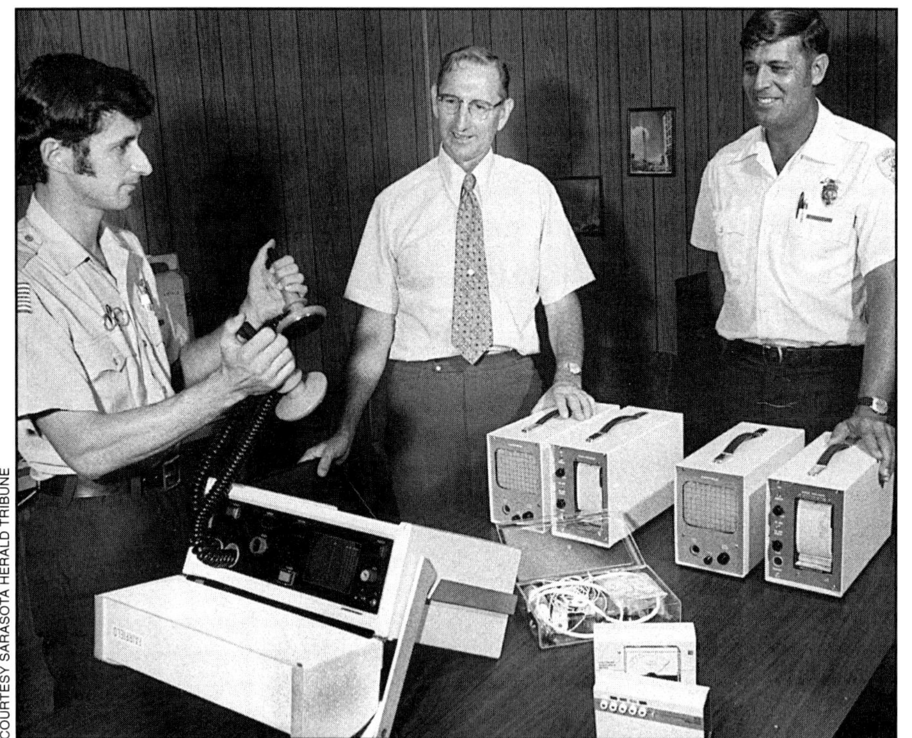

The department's first EGG Monitor/Defibrillator in 1973. In January 1974 EMT II Don Grant performed the first successful defibrillation outside a hospital in Sarasota. Left to right: Dennis Sargent, Chief Harold Stinchcomb, and Thomas Rhoades.

the importance of the rescue program and changed its name to the City of Sarasota Department of Fire-Rescue.[28]

Today's patients receive the best that training, technology, and caring personnel can provide. Patients are treated with equipment and procedures that would have been considered science fiction only a few years ago. Most patients are transported to Sarasota Memorial or Doctor's Hospital. Firefighters, EMT's, and paramedics work as a team whose actions are directed by the paramedic as a football team is directed by the quarterback. Patients suffering from critical medical ailments must be stabilized on scene prior to being transported. Essential treatment must not be delayed even to achieve a quick transport.

A 9-1-1 call received in CommCe, the department's dispatch center, illustrates the role of the emergency rescue team. An excited wife of a man in his fifties reported that her husband had just stopped breathing and was turning blue. An advanced life support rescue and an engine for additional personnel were immediately dispatched. Simultaneously, an emergency medical dispatcher instructed the wife over the telephone on how to administer cardiopulmonary resuscitation (CPR) to her husband. Her efforts continued until the sound of sirens stopped abruptly outside. Only four minutes had passed, but it certainly seemed like an eternity to her.

The team went to work with few words. A quick check revealed that the patient was not breathing and was without a pulse. A mask applied over the patient's face directed oxygen from the ventilator into the patient's lungs and soon the patient's chest began to rise and fall. The monitor defibrillator was prepared as the paramedics placed the metallic paddles on the patient's chest.

The monitor indicated that the heart was in ventricular fibrillation. The words "all clear" by the paramedic caused an instinctive reaction by the team: all hands were removed from the patient while 200

the emergency room physician. They have communicated directly with the physician and followed their orders. The primary difference between the treatment rendered by the physician and the paramedic has been the environment under which it was provided. The paramedic's work environment was not necessarily ideal. They worked in rain, cold, and the dark of night. They found their patients in burning buildings, entangled in vehicles, and submerged in water. They functioned regardless of the adversities they faced because a life depended on them. Over the years, their care has been increasingly appreciated as an asset that complements the definitive care provided by the physician.[27]

The Sarasota Fire Department has gone through a gradual metamorphosis over the years. The department originated from the need to protect the city from fire; to that end they have done an excellent job. But with every passing year the department's emphasis has shifted more towards rescue. In 1992, 61 percent of the department's emergencies were rescue related. The Sarasota Fire Department emerged from its fire cocoon in January of 1989 when it officially recognized

Paramedics and EMT's became the eyes and ears of the emergency room physician via medical radios.

joules of electricity passed through the patient's heart. Two additional shocks, each with increasing doses of electricity, were also unsuccessful. The crew was neither frustrated nor surprised and proceeded with their work as if the whole incident had been well rehearsed.

A firefighter compressed the patient's chest five times to each breath provided by the palm-sized ventilator. This synchronous effort by man and machine provided blood rich in essential oxygen to the patient's brain.

A bag of intravenous (IV) fluid was prepared while the paramedic inspected the arms of the patient for a suitable vein through which to administer medications. Seeing none, he had to rely on his anatomy training and blindly insert the needle where the vein should be located. Experience and training had proven effective as the needle was skillfully threaded into the vein. The needle was removed leaving a thin plastic catheter. A bag of fluid steadily dripped through a clear tubing which was connected to the catheter. The tubing provided an IV lifeline through which medications were injected.

Simultaneously, a second paramedic attempted to visualize the patient's vocal cords using a lighted instrument. Hampered by working in cramped quarters, poor lighting, and on the floor, he successfully located them and inserted a cuffed tube between them to protect the patient's airway.

The words "all clear" rang out again, and the patient was defibrillated again. The monitor began to show a rhythm, which was manually confirmed by feeling the patient's pulse. The wife's face showed signs of relief, but relief was not yet mirrored by the crew. Yes, the heart was beating, but dangerously slow. Still other medications were injected to increase the heart-rate, all without result.

The paramedic readied the pacemaker feature of the monitor-defibrillator and placed two electrodes on the patient's chest. With the push of a button, the patients heart rate doubled and his color improved from an ashen grey to a normal pink. As the crew placed him on the stretcher, he began to breathe of his own accord, but they continued to provide assistance.

Twenty-five minutes after the crew began their work, they wheeled the patient to the rescue unit as his wife was seated in the front seat. Five minutes later all arrived at Sarasota Memorial Hospital. The wife was escorted to the admitting clerk, and the patient was greeted with another flurry of attention as nurses and the emergency room physician continued the patient care. Nearly two weeks later the patient was released from the hospital to a tearful and jubilant family reunion. Although the man had never met his rescuers, they had touched his life in a very special way. They had given him a second chance at life.

Paramedics touch many lives and are called upon to wear many hats during their career. In a days work they may function as rescuers, firefighters, counselors, teachers, students, guardians, and friends. Perhaps the most important role of the paramedic is as care giver. Caring is the force that drives a paramedic who has worked a busy twenty-four hour shift to reassuringly hold the hand of an elderly patient. The paramedic cares enough to put a second blanket on the patient before taking them into the cool night air. They can still produce a friendly smile when putting a fallen patient back to bed at four o'clock in the morning or produce a teddy bear to ease the fear of an ill child. They treat their patients as if they were members of their own family. Many calls require simple procedures and a human touch. Others require urgent intervention. In their own heart, paramedics share the patient's pain and anxiety but do not always have the luxury to display these emotions because the burden of time sometimes weighs heavily on the patient's chance of survival. It is this genuine concern for people that has attracted most paramedics to this profession and continues to drive them day by day. Their reward comes in knowing that they have lessened someone's suffering or even saved a life. It is a bittersweet profession unlike any other.

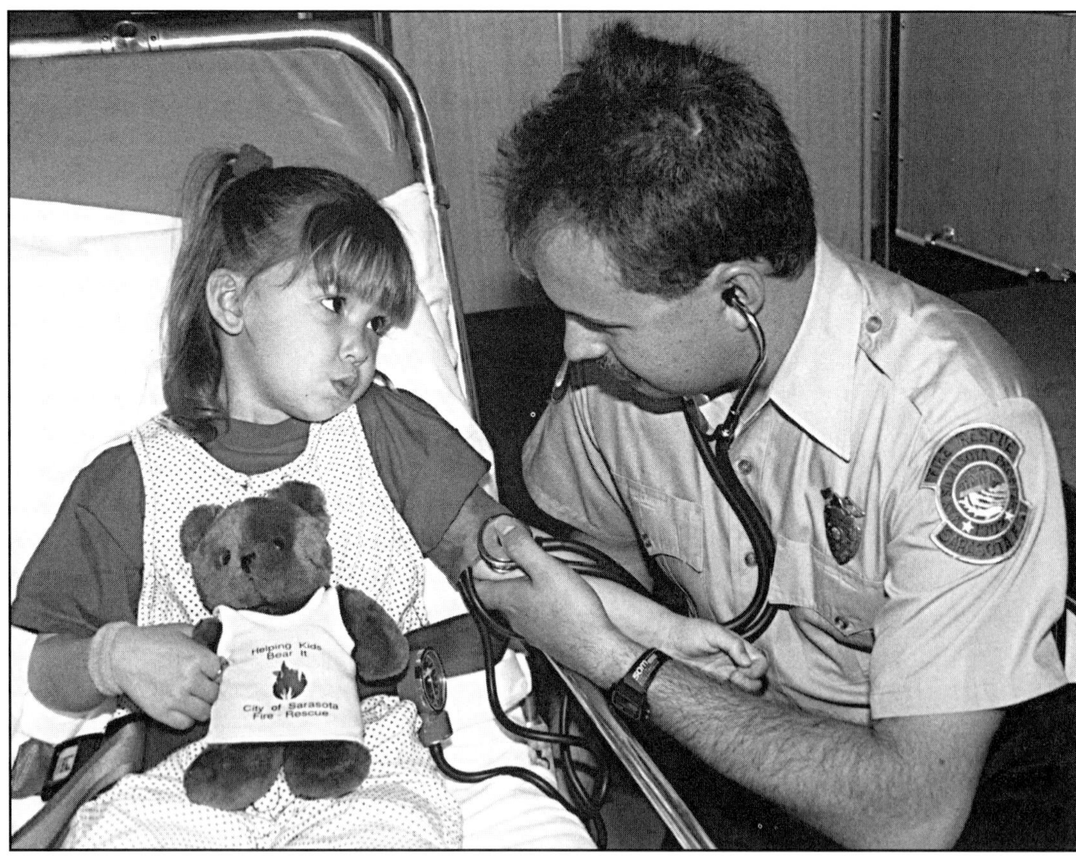

Paramedic Dan Dahlberg wins the trust of five-year old Rachel Watson.

COURTESY WAYNE A. WELSH

CHAPTER 19

THE GOLDEN HOUR: TRAUMA CARE

The term "golden hour" was originally coined by Dr. R Adams Cowley of the Maryland Institute for Emergency Medical Services, who is regarded as the pioneer of modern trauma care. Dr. Cowley advocated that most trauma patients die of shock, which comes from sluggish or non-existent circulation and the resulting chemical changes in the body. He believed that most trauma patients could be saved if he could stop the bleeding and restore blood pressure within one hour. Patients who have experienced shock for more than one hour will likely die. Surgical intervention within that one hour, therefore, is critical for increasing the patient's chance of survival. This hour — called the golden hour — begins the moment the injury occurs.[1]

Sarasota's paramedics, EMT's and firefighters strive to shave minutes and seconds off the rescue time in order to preserve the golden hour. Their equipment is designed for safety, function, and speed, and they diligently train to improve their efficiency. This emphasis is vividly depicted by a recent vehicle accident in the City of Sarasota. Two vehicles driving through the night streets collided with an almost deafening impact that was heard for blocks away. The occupants were trapped in a tangled mass of metal and broken glass. The patients possessed varying degrees of injuries. One critically injured occupant remained unconscious; this patient's golden hour had begun.

CommCe received the call through the 9-1-1 emergency line six minutes after the accident occurred. The caller reported a two car accident with people trapped inside. The station alarm and lights were triggered by

CommCe. The crews jumped to their feet and scrambled to get dressed while listening intently to the dispatch information. Although they had been soundly sleeping only one minute before, they now maneuvered cautiously through the city streets. As the apparatus approached the scene, the crimson reflection of the beacons projected an ominous hue on the shattered windshield of the cars. The first ten minutes of the golden hour had already slipped away.

The first units to arrive on scene were the rescue unit, fire engine, and hazardous materials truck. Each person had a specific function and proceeded immediately. The rescue crew primarily provided patient care. The engine crew immediately extended a hose line to protect the patients and rescuers in case a fire resulted from the leaking gasoline. The hazardous materials crew prepared the hydraulic extrication equipment commonly known as the "jaws of life." The paramedic assessed the patients and reported that one patient was in critical condition and required helicopter transport directly to a trauma center. The remaining patients were not as seriously injured and could go by ambulance to the local hospital. He requested CommCe to issue a trauma alert, thus warning the trauma center of the impending patient arrival and requesting a helicopter. Additional rescue teams and the shift battalion chief were also called to respond.

The patients in the second vehicle were not trapped but required cautious handling by the incoming rescue crews since improper handling of potential neck and back injuries could result in permanent disabilities.

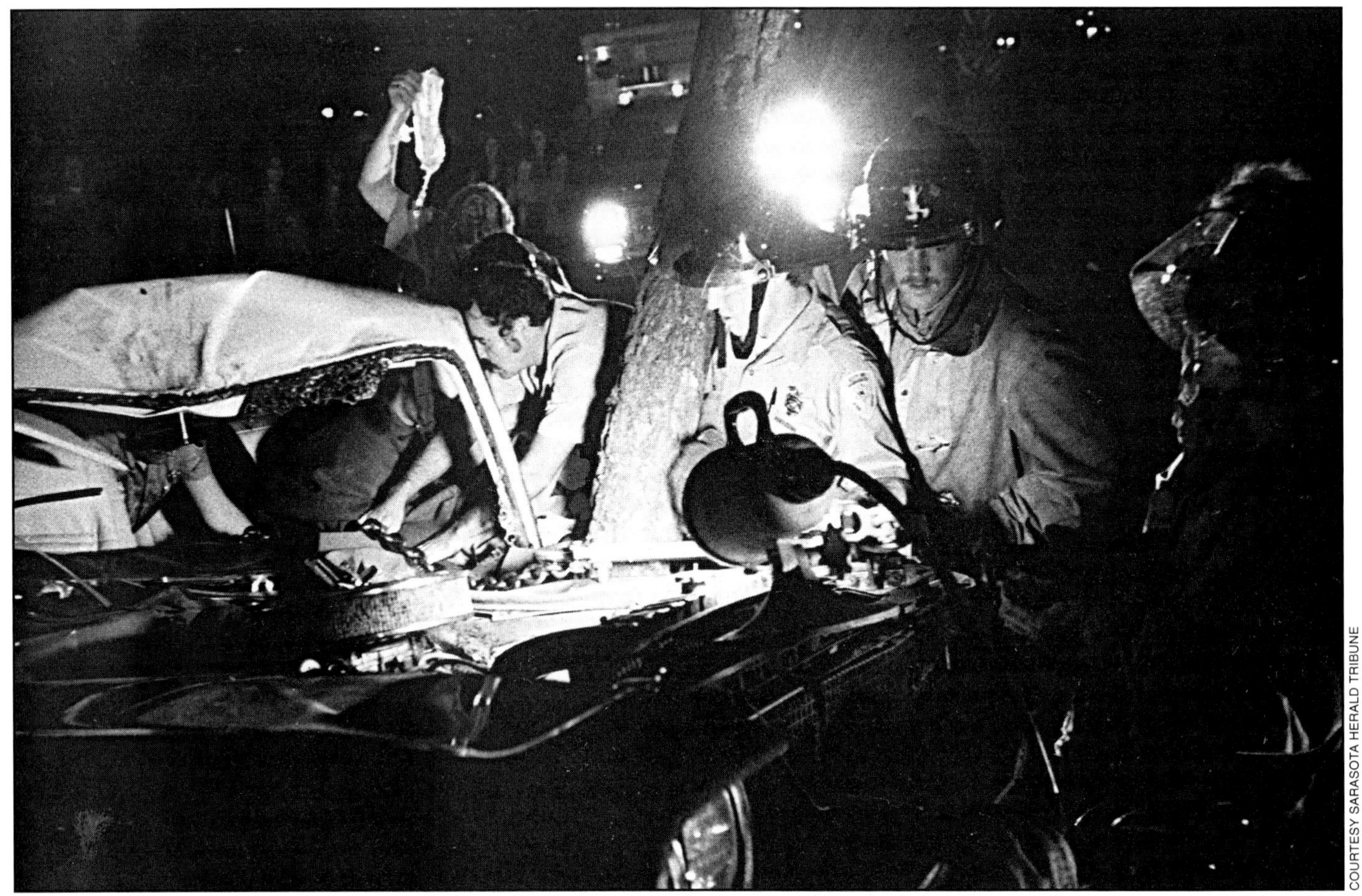

Firefighters, Paramedics and EMT's work feverishly to extricate the victims of a vehicle accident in the early 1970's. The victims receive emergency care while firefighters disentangle them from the vehicle.

Soon rescuers realized that it would be difficult to extricate the critical patient. The front of the vehicle had crumbled, pushing the dashboard and steering wheel downward upon his chest and legs. The doors on both the drivers and passengers side were so badly damaged that they could not open.

An EMT climbed into the vehicle through a broken window. He immobilized the patient's head and neck using his hands while closely monitoring the patient's pulse and breathing. Both the EMT and the patient were covered with a blanket to protect them from flying glass while the work ensued.

All the windows in the vehicle were broken out or removed to prevent them from unpredictably shattering and injuring either the rescuers or the patient. Hydraulic cutters then sliced each of the posts supporting the car's roof using sixty thousand pounds of cutting force. After the rescuers cut all the posts, they lifted the roof from the car and placed it safely out of the working area.

Simultaneously, firefighters operated the hydraulic spreaders to remove the vehicle doors. The controlled displacement of metal allowed the firefighters to free the doors' hinges and locking mechanism. They could then fully access the patient, but he was still held captive by the steering wheel and dashboard. The extrication continued as the paramedic administered oxygen to the patient and established two IV life-lines.

Cuts were made at the base of the driver's and passenger's door frames to create a hinged effect. A hydraulic cylinder called a ram was used to pivot the entire front end of the vehicle forward. The vehicle bent at the cuts, creating the sound of straining metal. Soon the entire front of the vehicle had tilted forward, bringing the dash and steering wheel with it. The patient was rapidly packaged to prevent further injury to his spine while he was removed from the vehicle.

The patient was loaded into the rescue unit while a

glance at his watch told the paramedic that half of the patient's golden hour was already gone. The rescue team proceeded cutting the patient's clothes off and examining him from head to toe for injuries. The primary injuries seemed to be fractured ribs, legs, and internal bleeding in the abdomen. A tube was inserted into his airway to assist his labored breathing. Two IV's were established and the mast suit, an inflatable pair of trousers were applied to assist the patient's failing circulatory system. The rescue team, awaiting the arrival of the helicopter, worked feverishly to stabilize the patient.

Strobe lights were placed in the street to mark the perimeter of the helicopter landing zone. Police and fire apparatus were positioned to block traffic. The distinctive sound of helicopter rotors slicing the air and the vibration of the rescue unit from the wind created by the helicopter alerted the rescue crew that Bayflight had arrived. Information, paperwork, and finally the patient was transferred to Bayflight's flight-nurse and flight-medic while the pilot kept a watchful eye on the craft and weather conditions.

Bayflight departed enroute to Bayfront Medical Center in St. Petersburg, a level II trauma center. The patient arrived at the trauma center fourteen minutes later and was met at the door by a trauma surgeon. He was whisked into surgery with still ten minutes remaining to his golden hour. The immediate availability of a surgeon justified the flight to the trauma center when other hospitals were just minutes away. Rapid surgical intervention and not mere entrance into a hospital saves the lives of traumatically injured patients. In this case, the patient survived his ordeal thanks to the team effort of the entire Emergency Medical System.

CHAPTER 20

MOVING FORWARD TOGETHER

Thomas Fields was appointed the sixth chief of the Sarasota Fire Department on December 28, 1988. His interest in the fire service was sparked at an early age by his father, Marshall. Marshall was an avid fire buff who respected and befriended the firefighters in his home town of Maysville, Kentucky.[1]

Tom fondly remembers accompanying his father to watch firefighters extinguish blazes in Maysville. Father and son stood across the street and watched the action with all the excitement of a major league ball game. When the fire was extinguished and the hose picked up, one of the firefighters surprised five year-old Tom and lifted him to the front seat of the engine. All the way back to the station Tom rang the engine's bell, a sound which never left his imagination. The same firefighter, who was like an uncle to Tom, was killed in the line of duty years later. But Tom never lost his love for the fire service; he made application and was employed by the Sarasota Fire Department on November 29, 1966.

When Chief Fields took the reigns of the fire department in 1988, he instituted his business style of management. After all, he ran a ten million dollar a year business. Fields also took on the issue of firefighter safety, which was a concern both locally and nationally. Tragically, one out of three career firefighters nationally were injured in the line of duty in 1991, making firefighting the most dangerous profession in the United States. During the same year, 32 firefighters gave the ultimate sacrifice, their lives. The city of Sarasota, on the other hand, has never lost a firefighter in the line of duty, a record which attests to the quality of their training and fire prevention efforts.[2]

The department made national headlines on August 8, 1989 for extinguishing an early morning blaze at the Ringling School of Art and Design. Named after the circus magnate John Ringling, the school has become one of the top art schools in the country. The series of buildings that house the school, previously known as the Bay Haven Hotel, were constructed in 1926. The first firefighters who arrived on scene were confronted with a tremendous body of fire that had already burned out the side windows and blown out the front ones. The radiant heat and flames were moving toward several adjacent buildings in the historic complex. Firefighters initially made an aggressive interior attack hoping to stop the fire quickly but fire had already entered the attic. They were forced to retreat when the ceiling began to collapse upon them. Firefighters hurriedly set up exterior hoselines and poured thousands of gallons of water per minute into the fire. Quick action and intrepid firefighting prevented the spread of fire beyond the building of origin. Although the building that served as the cafeteria and classrooms was destroyed, the remainder of the school was saved and opened on schedule for the semester. Chief Thomas Fields said, "The firefighters made a great stop on the fire. They saved a national landmark."[3]

Chief Fields eliminated the previous practice of responding to emergencies in fire apparatus staffed by only one firefighter. Even though additional units might also respond, a lone firefighter could be in grave danger. This not only improved safety for firefighters but the quality of service provided to the public. The department also implemented a program in which a designated physician would provide medical physicals to each employee. He would also be available for consultation, testing, and treatment of employees after exposures to infectious diseases or hazardous materials. Many of the department's fire apparatus were also replaced with engines that offered greater firefighting capabilities and improved safety. The newest apparatus, a Pierce engine, features a totally enclosed six-person cab to protect firefighters and deliver them safely to the emergency scene and back to the station. The practice of firefighters riding on the tailboards of apparatus was discontinued in the early 1980's due to safety concerns. Even the 50 foot aerial ladder and 1000 gallon per minute nozzle of the new engine can be operated using a remote control, thus allowing firefighters to battle fires from a position of relative safety when dealing with situations that offer a high degree of danger or probability of explosion.

Safety is also a vital concern when dealing with chemicals. An abundance of chemicals in the commu-

nity, if improperly handled, burn, explode, give off radiation, or have other harmful or toxic effects to humans. When they escape their effects can be disastrous. Some materials even explode if exposed to water. The department answered the community's need for an organized response to hazardous materials incidents. They accepted delivery of a vehicle dedicated to the response to hazardous material incidents in 1983 with the creation of the Hazardous Incident Tactical (H.I.T.) team. The H.I.T. team responds in a specially designed vehicle. The vehicle, which was purchased in 1992, was equipped with an on-board computer system capable of providing detailed information about chemicals and their behavior. This information is used to handle hazardous materials incidents in a safe and organized manner. Hazardous materials, high level rescues, and entrapments are examples of the difficult operations team members are specially trained to handle.

The fire department teamed up with the police department to assist with other types of difficult operations. The fire department provided three firefighter-paramedics in 1985 to cooperatively work with

Three generations of fire chiefs. Chief Thomas Fields (left) passes command of the Bureau of Fire-Rescue to newly appointed Chief Julius E. Halas (center) while Retired Chief Harold Stinchcomb provides moral support.

the Special Weapons and Tactics (S.W.A.T.) team. They respond with the S.W.A.T. team to volatile police incidents such as drug raids, hostages, or snipers. They provide immediate medical assistance to police officers and citizens who are injured during a police incident. These S.W.A.T. medics have all attended the Law Enforcement Minimum Standards training and are reserve police officers. They were provided intensive training in police procedures and use of weapons. The S.W.A.T. medics have been armed should they need to defend themselves or a fellow police officer.

The fire department has worked diligently over the years to keep pace with the growth that occurred in the city of Sarasota. Apparatus and manpower were steadily increased as well as the types and levels of services provided. In recent years Sarasota has felt the effects of a floundering national economy. As a result tourism suffered, local and state tax revenue fell, and the city stopped receiving federal revenue sharing funds. Unwilling to raise local taxes, the city commission has looked for other options to make ends meet.

One option considered was to consolidate the city of Sarasota and Sarasota county into a single county-wide fire department. Feasibility studies were conducted by the Insurance Services Office and local government. Many of the barriers to consolidation were methodically removed by both departments. Ultimately, it was a four million dollar shortfall that prevented the two fire departments from uniting.

The city commission chose instead to consolidate fire and police into a department of public safety. Firefighters and police officers have retained their identity and normal job functions. Divisions such as training, administrative, and service combined to create a theoretical cost savings. A critical step in obtaining these savings was the elimination of a number of management positions through normal attrition as a result of retirements. "Rightsizing" became the buzzword to describe the reduction in staff and apparatus. Seemingly the city could no longer afford to bear the fiscal burden of the department under the current economic conditions. A number of programs fell prey to rightsizing. Programs such as public CPR training and the department's weekly educational television show called Fireline were eliminated. Other programs such as the fire inspections of commercial buildings have been transferred to the city's building department. The city commission's decision to rightsize the department most assuredly will save money. The overriding question remains: will an increase in lives lost or property damage result? It may be years before Sarasota feels the true impact of rightsizing.

The new department of public safety was created on October 14, 1992. It included both the bureau of fire-rescue and the bureau of police. Julius E. Halas was appointed as the chief of fire-rescue services bureau.

Thomas Fields retired on February 28, 1993. Fields said he will miss the personal challenge he experienced in the fire service. "Every firefighter must at some time ask themself, Do I have the guts to handle the situation?" Fields, who proved himself in both the fireground and the political arena said, "The one thing I will miss most is the comradery among firefighters. Everyone is happy together, sad together, we laugh together and mourn together. We are like an extended family."

CHAPTER 21

EXCELLENCE AND PRIDE

The 1990's proved to be a challenging time for the bureau of fire-rescue, a time when they had to do more — with less. After his retirement, Chief Fields relinquished command of the bureau to Julius E. Halas on October 14, 1992. Halas, only 38 years old, was the seventh chief in Sarasota's history. He immediately implemented his participative style of management. Halas joined the bureau on September 23, 1974 seeking the financial security and long term career opportunity that the bureau had to offer.[1]

Halas assisted with the reorganization which combined the department of fire-rescue and the department of police into a single entity as the department of public safety. The scope of the reorganization was expanded through the influence and participation of the Sarasota-Manatee Professional Firefighters and Paramedics Union, local 2546. The union is an advocate of firefighter rights and safety. Halas facilitated the removal of an engine and an aerial apparatus from active service resulting in a cost savings to the city. The remaining apparatus and personnel were redistributed to maximize their response efficiency. Ironically, these cost-cutting measures resulted in an improved rating of a level two from the Insurance Services Office and a subsequent savings on fire insurance premiums to businesses operating in the city.

It seems the city of Sarasota and many others across the country have developed a new philosophy about fire protection which has resulted from the flattening of the national economy. Fire departments no longer prepare to handle major incidents sometimes known as "the big one." Instead they develop their armament of apparatus and personnel to handle the normal complement of incidents.

Departments rely on mutual aid assistance from neighboring communities and networking with other departments for large scale incidents such as the seven alarm fire in July of 1993 at "The Recycling Place," a newspaper recycling plant. The city of Sarasota as well as a number of neighboring departments responded to assist Sarasota County control a fire that could have expanded to devastating proportions and caused loss of lives.

The city and county of Sarasota have been mutually developing plans for an automatic aid agreement which calls for firefighters to respond across city-county boundaries. Responses would be based on the closest available units rather than jurisdictional boundaries.

The issue of consolidation of the city and county fire departments was raised in 1992 by the City Commission. Although consolidation of the two departments did not occur, it is an issue that will likely recur in upcoming years as a result of changing commissioners and the need to further pursue cost reductions. Some city residents, however, feared they would lose control of the actual location and quantity of the department's resources. A number of recent changes have taken place which align the two departments towards a common destiny. Two of those changes involve aspects of training and communications.

The "burn building" owned and operated by Sarasota County Technical Institute is used to challenge and train fire service personnel throughout the area. A variety of actual fire scenarios can be created within the structure providing quality training which prepares firefighters for actual emergencies.

The city of Sarasota has discontinued running firefighter recruit schools at its training academy. Instead, Sarasota County Technical Institute (S.C.T.I.) assumed that role and provides a great deal of the refresher firefighter training received by both the city of Sarasota and Sarasota county firefighters. S.C.T.I. completed the construction of a three story burn building in 1991 which is used by firefighters from throughout the area. Firefighters confront actual fires inside the structure and therefore remain prepared for actual emergencies. The burn building is state of the art and was designed with firefighter safety in mind. The fires are supplied by LPG and firefighters are viewed through a control room while temperatures and the internal atmosphere are electronically monitored and controlled. The burn building is located at 400 N. Beneva Road and is one of the most modern in the United States.

In addition to training issues, planned changes in communications are also bringing the city and county fire departments closer together. Sarasota county has begun designing a new communications center which will adequately serve their communications needs for the next decade and provide room to grow for the next twenty years. This new center will operate using the 800 megahertz trunking system which utilizes available radio frequencies to their maximum efficiency by computer coordination. This improved technology is costly but will improve the quality of communications which is important to firefighters. Their lives depend on receiving messages such as, "Evacuate the building, the roof is about to collapse."[2]

It is proposed that the center will replace the myriad of 18 different radio systems used for fire, police, emergency management, mosquito control, etc., and the 3700 individual government radio users in the city and county. CommCe most likely will see the sun set as it closes its doors after being in operation since 1971. The new center is projected to begin operations in 1995.[3]

Consolidated efforts in both training and communications do not assure that consolidation into a single county-wide fire department will occur but they certainly remove some of the obstacles. Changes in the county's method of collecting fire taxes have further aligned the two departments. The state of the economy and the make-up of the city and county commissions will likely determine the future of consolidation.

Meanwhile, the city commission grappled to balance the 1993-1994 budget. In an unprecedented move, they considered laying-off seven firefighters, EMT's, and paramedics. This reduction in personnel to an already downsized department would have resulted in the removal of additional apparatus. The impact to city residents can only be speculated. Fortunately, the early retirement of a few senior fire officers averted lay-offs but still resulted in slightly reduced staffing.

Regardless of the political and financial burdens the city and department must face, every 9-1-1 call will continue to be answered by a team of well trained and motivated individuals who have dedicated their lives to helping those in need. Whenever a fire or medical

Firefighters demonstrate the use of the life net on Students' Day.

emergency strikes a family and they are at their worst, Sarasota's firefighters shine and give their best. Modern management theory subscribes that the most valuable asset of any organization is its people. If this is true, the future of the City of Sarasota Bureau of Fire-Rescue is bright. Twenty-four hours a day, 365 days a year, WE SERVE WITH EXCELLENCE AND PRIDE!

"WE SERVE WITH EXCELLENCE AND PRIDE"

The firefighters of today's City of Sarasota Bureau of Fire-Rescue share a proud heritage. It is easy to believe that the fire department is composed of glistening fire trucks, expansive stations, flashing lights and screaming sirens. Nothing could be further from the truth. These things are merely tools of the trade just as a hammer and anvil are tools of the blacksmith trade. The Sarasota Fire Department and its firefighters are synonymous. It is the firefighters that invest the sweat labor, endure blistering heat, push themselves beyond the point of exhaustion, witness tragedies, and risk their lives for the citizens they serve. They indeed are the department.

The following salaried firefighters have served the city of Sarasota for one year or more.

Adams, Frank	Burkert, Keith	Dogoda, Anthony E., Jr.	Gingras, John Sr.
Addy, Clarence	Burzenski, James	Donovan, Jack	Glanden, John
Albritton, Curtis D.	Cain, Roy	Douthit, Peter F.	Gohl, Jeffrey K.
Alston, Jerry L.	Cameron, George R.	Drumright, Arthur	Gore, William
Ambrozic, John F., Jr.	Cameron, Stanley	Eckerd, Clayton	Grant, Donald H.
Aubin, William P.	Campbell, Bruce A.	Edmonds, David R.	Greer, Earl B.
Austin, Richard K.	Carlin, William	Elliott, Charles	Grubbs, Wayne R.
Baber, Lewis	Carlson, Hugh V.	Elliott, Neal B.	Gueli, Jeffrey G.
Barrow, James	Carlton, Robert	Emmerich, Patrick	Haehle, Ronald
Barry, Gerald	Carriero, John J.	Enos, James C.	Hager, Melvin O.
Beattie, Timothy R.	Cassidy, Norman	Enos, Leon	Haisley, Gerry L.
Beauchamp, Brian W.	Cave, Ernest F., Jr.	Faltz, James	Halas, Julius E.
Beauchamp, William J., Jr.	Chase, Thomas K.	Feraci, Angelo	Hanlon, John G.
Behrens, Henry	Chiesa, Roberto P.	Fields, William T.	Harper, Patrick G.
Bell, W. W.	Clark, Chris	Fismer, Carl	Hartley, Michael S.
Bell, Willis L.	Clemons, Harvey	Flanagan, Robert	Hartman, William
Bennett, William G.	Coffman, Daniel L.	Fralick, Rufus	Hay, John C.
Best, William J.	Cogar, Gary L.	Frazier, James L.	Hedgeman, Emanuel C.
Bilter, Hugo	Conley, Robert M.	Frey, Matthew	Heggs, Darren
Black, James Jr.	Cordasco, Joseph F.	Friend, Elbert E.	Hernandez, Vincent
Bock, William	Corwin, Larry	Frosch, Larry A.	Hibbs, Brian R.
Bonsignore, Randy	Cote, Exor Jr.	Fryer, Vernon	Higashi, Wade K.
Boutieller, Mary I.	Cowsert, James	Funk, Larry	Hildreth, Keith D.
Bouwman, Sandra J.	Craig, Donnie	Futch, David	Hobbs, Patrik
Boyette, Joseph W.	Dahlberg, Daniel R.	Gabbert, James F.	Hood, Phillip Mose
Braun, Keith	Davidson, Richard	Gabbert, Tate	Hoover, Donald
Bridwell, Lawrence	Denham, Thomas C.	Gamble, Donald L.	Hosfeld, Dale
Briggs, Darren L.	Denner, Francis H., III	Garrison, Gregory T.	House, Christopher D.
Brooks, Juan	Derr, Robert	Gerardi, Craig J.	Howell, William W.
Broom, Thomas J.	Devaughn, Eric W.	Gibilian, Charles	Howells, Terrance
Bulger, Stephen A.	Dillon, Kevin	Gilmore, Donnie L.	Hull, E.J.
Bullard, Robert	Doane, Alden	Gingras, John P., Jr.	Jackson, George M.

Jackson, James
Jackson, John P., Jr.
James, Ricky
Jenkins, Charlena S.
Jarrett, James F.
Johnson, Saul
Johnston, Charles W.
Johnston, James
Jones, James C.
Jones, Melvin
Jones, Mark
Joseph, Charles W.
Joyner, Murray
Kall, Stephen C.
Karako, Gerald
Karnes, Willis
Kendrick, Stephen S.
Kennedy, Kenneth
Ketchum, Samuel R.
Kidd, W. Wayne
King, R. II
Knowles, H.M. Jr.
Knowles, H.M.
Knowles, James G.
Lamb, Robert P.
Lang, Ted C.
Lanier, Alfred
Larrow, Frank
Lawrence, Marion
Lawton, John S.
Leighton, William P.
Lemmon, Jon
Light, Al J.
Light, Charles K.
Loehr, Gregory H.
Lopez, Jimmy
Love, Anthony
Manson, Otto
Mankin, Phillip
Marinelli, Carl Jr.
Marsh, L. Cody
Martin, Darryl
Martin, John
Martinez, Eugenio A.
Martino, Michael J.
Maus, George
May, Thomas R.

Mayo, George
Mayo, Sherman
McAdoo, Steven W.
McLaughlin, Bruce
McLeod, Robert L. Jr.
McLeod, Robert L. III
McCord, James
McGee, Lloyd Vernon
McGinnis, Richard
McGrath, Robert A.
McKeon, William
McKinney, Jimmy R.
McKinnon, James
Menzies, Chris
Meyer, Charles
Mikronis, Edgar A.
Miller, Albert
Miller, Edwin B.
Molmberg, William
Molter, Jacob
Morgan, Lewis
Morse, David
Moyer, John
Olsen, Robert A.
Opitz, Charles
Ormond, Robbin W.
Oswalt, Dale E.
Paige, Roderick A.
Paraino, Donald
Parsons, Ralph
Paulus, Chester J.
Petellat, A.J.
Petellat, Robert F.
Peterson, Richard
Pike, Donald
Pohumek, Eugene
Potter, Robert G.
Powers, Vernon
Prestia, Daniel
Pritchard, Charles
Putnam, Eric
Radford, John
Rayner, William
Rebar, George
Regnier, Michael J.
Reid, Douglas J.
Rieser, Alan W.

Rhoades, Steve
Rhoades, Thomas J.
Rhoades, Thomas T. Jr.
Richardson, Keith A.
Robb, Richard
Roberts, Richard
Robins, Peter W.
Robinson, John
Robinson, Ralph
Roby, Raymond N.
Rode, Hans R.
Rodoski, Michael T.
Roland, John
Rosa, Anthony L.
Rush, Larry K.
Sargent, Dennis
Schlabach, William
Schultz, William
Schuster, James R.
Scutari, A.R.
Sebor, Jack R.
Shealy, Timothy
Shealy, James
Shorter, Russell
Shyne, Susan M.
Sims, Glover K.
Sliter, Roger A.
Smith, Gary
Smith, Paul
Snow, Scott T.
Stanfield, Roy
Stegge, Gregory J.
Stephens, Clarence I.
Stershic, David J.
Stevens, John H.
Steverson, John
Stinchcomb, Harold
Stone, John
Stoudt, Franklin A.
Stulce, Randall R.
Suarez, Michael K.
Sumner, James
Tatum, William
Taylor, Elmer
Taylor, Glennon
Taylor, John
Teate, Carlton

Terrell, Cynthia L.
Terry, Roger
Thibodeau, Daniel T.
Thomas, Byron K.
Thomas, Braille B.
Thomas, Vincent R.
Thorne, Mitchell D.
Thorson, Ronald
Tokarski, Darrell R.
Trefethen, Mark G.
Troyer, Aden
Tucker, David
Tucker, William
Turvey, Donald
Tuttle, Mark C.
Vowell, Robert
Wagner, William
Walker, Boyd
Walker, Wiley
Wallers, Vernon
Walp, Mahlon
Ward, Allen
Watson, Kent A.
Weir, Fred
Weldon, William Jr.
Welsh, Wayne A.
Werstler, Terry
Wessels, Ernest
Weston, Ronald W.
Williams, Bret A.
Williams, Dennis
Williams, Richard
Wilson, Philip R.
Woods, James A., Sr.
Woomert, Larry
Yahraus, Kenneth C.
Yahraus, Michael K.
Yauilla, Charles
Young, Michael S.
Zeigler, Doyle
Zelonis, Bill A.
Ziegenfelder, Wm.

Notes

Chapter 1. A Place to Call Home

1   Board of Trade, Sarasota, Florida, *Information Relative To Sarasota*, Florida, undated, p. 1.
2   A.K. Whitaker, *One Man's Family*, 19 March 1969, Sarasota County Department of Historical Resources, part I, pp. 1,2.
3   Ibid.
4   Charlie Briggs, *One Hundred Years Ago/Old-Time Sarasota*, (Sarasota: Jere Parker, 1986), p.8.
5   Whitaker/ Stewart Family Collection, Sarasota County Department of Historical Resources.
6   Whitaker, *One Man's Family*, part II, p. 3.
7   Ibid., part I, pp. 3,4.
8   Mae Wilson, "Whitakers Figure In Sarasota Story," *Sarasota Herald Tribune*, 28 Oct. 1959.
9   Ibid.
10 Whitaker, *One Man's Family*, part I, p. 4.

Chapter 2. On the Warpath

1   *Harper's Weekly*, 12 June 1858, p. 376.
2   Ibid.
3   Karl H. Grismer, *The Story of Sarasota* (Tampa, Florida Grower Press, 1946), p. 37.
4   Emma C. Humphries, "In Woman's World," *The Manatee River Journal*, 18 Dec. 1913.
5   Grismer, *The Story of Sarasota*, p. 37.
6   Ibid., pp. 37, 38.
7   Mae Wilson, "Whitakers Figure In Sarasota Story," *The Sarasota Herald Tribune*, 28 Oct. 1959.
8   Grismer, *The Story of Sarasota*, p. 38.
9   Ibid.
10 Emma C. Humphries, "In Woman's World," *The Manatee River Journal*, 18 Dec. 1913.
11 Edna Mosely Landers, *Biography of Mary Wyatt Whitaker*, Sarasota County Department of Historical Resources, Whitaker Collection.
12 Gene M. Burnett, *Florida's Past* (Englewood, Pineapple Press, 1986), p. 36.
13 Grismer, *The Story of Sarasota*, p. 38.
14 Landers, *Biography of Mary Wyatt Whitaker*.
15 Grismer, *The Story of Sarasota*, p. 39.
16 Ibid., p. 39.
17 Emma C. Humphries, "In Woman's World," *The Manatee River Journal*, 18 Dec. 1913.
18 Mae Wilson, "Whitakers Figure In Sarasota Story," *The Sarasota Herald Tribune*, 28 Oct. 1959.
19 *Harper's Weekly*, 12 June 1858, p. 376.
20 Grismer, *The Story of Sarasota*, p. 39.
21 Whitaker, *One Man's Family*, part I, p. 5.
22 Grismer, *The Story of Sarasota*, p. 40.
23 Ibid.
24 Whitaker, *One Man's Family*, part I, pp. 5, 6.
25 Lillie B. McDuffee, *The Lures of Manatee* (Atlanta, Georgia, Foote and Davies, Third Edition), p. 142.
26 Ibid.

Chapter 3. From the Ground Up

1   Guy Paschal, *A Vivid History of Sarasota*, p. 45.
2   Grismer, *The Story of Sarasota*, p. 101.
3   Del Marth, *Yesterday's Sarasota* (Sarasota, Lindsay Curtis Publishing Co., 1973), pp. 16-19.
4   Ibid, pp. 18, 19.
5   Grismer, *The Story of Sarasota*, p. 101.
6   Alex Browning, *Browning Family Manuscript*, Sarasota County Department of Historical Resources, 21 March 1932, pp. 27-33.
7   Briggs, *One Hundred Years Ago/Old-Time Sarasota*.
8   Ibid.

Chapter 3 *(Continued)*

9   Marth, *Yesterday's Sarasota*, p. 19.
10 Browning, *Browning Family Manuscript*, pp. 27-33.
11 Ibid.
12 Marth, *Yesterday's Sarasota*, p. 21.
13 Briggs, *One Hundred Years Ago/Old-Time Sarasota*.
14 Grismer, *The Story of Sarasota*, pp. 101-102.
15 Browning, *Browning Family Manuscript*, pp. 27-33.
16 Ibid.
17 Marth, *Yesterday's Sarasota*, pp. 19-25.
18 Ibid., pp. 19, 21.
19 Ibid., p. 19.
20 Browning, *Browning Family Manuscript*, pp. 32, 61-62.
21 Grismer, *The Story of Sarasota*, pp. 103-104.
22 Marth, *Yesterday's Sarasota*, p. 19.
23 Browning, *Browning Family Manuscript*, p. 31.
24 Ibid.
25 Grismer, *The Story of Sarasota*, pp. 103-104.
26 Browning, *Browning Family Manuscript*, pp. 22-27.
27 Briggs, *One Hundred Years Ago/Old-Time Sarasota*.
28 Grismer, *The Story of Sarasota*, p. 102.

Chapter 4. Built to Burn

1   *Ordinances of the Town of Sarasota*, (Tampa: Tribune Print, 1903), 1-34.
2   Ibid.
3   Ibid.
4   "Another Fire: The Bradley Stables," *The Sarasota Times*, 10 Feb. 1910.
5   Rotha Harvey Matson, interview, Sarasota, 28 Jan. 1993.
6   City of Sarasota, *Minutes of Town Council*, 14 March 1911, Book 1, p. 429.
7   *Ordinances of the Town of Sarasota*, 1903, 1-34.
8   Ibid.
9   "Another Fire: The Bradley Stables," *The Sarasota Times*, 10 Feb. 1910.
10 "Permission By Mayor," *The Sarasota Times*, 7 Dec. 1911.
11 *Ordinances of the Town of Sarasota*, 1903, 1-34.
12 Ibid.
13 Ibid.
14 "Only Fireproof Buildings on Bay," *The Sarasota Times*, 11 June 1914.
15 *Ordinances of the Town of Sarasota*, 8 Sept. 1909, Ordinance No. 34, Book 1, pp. 104-107.
16 Ibid.

Chapter 5. Buckets and Brawn

1   "Bay View House Fire," *The Sarasota Times*, 10 Feb. 1910.
2   Ibid.
3   "Two Fires at Sarasota," *Manatee River Journal*, 10 Feb. 1910.
4   "Bay View House Fire," *The Sarasota Times*, 10 Feb. 1910.
5   Mr. Ron Norman, interview, Sarasota, 12 April 1991.
6   *The City of Cincinnati and Its Resources*, The Cincinnati Times Star Co., 1891, p. 145.
7   "Bay View House Fire," *The Sarasota Times*, 10 Feb. 1910.
8   Ibid.
9   Ibid.
10 Ibid.
11 Ibid.
12 Ibid.
13 "Another Fire: The Bradley Stables," *The Sarasota Times*, 10 Feb. 1910.
14 Ibid.
15 Ibid.
16 Ibid.

CHAPTER 6. WALK BEFORE YOU RUN

1 "Town Council Meets," *The Sarasota Times*, 20 Oct. 1910.
2 "Town Council Meets," *The Sarasota Times*, 10 Nov. 1910.
3 "Council Orders Improvements," *The Sarasota Times*, 29 Dec. 1910.
4 City of Sarasota, *Meeting of Town Council*, 6 Dec. 1910, Book 1, P. 416.
5 "Council Orders Improvements," *The Sarasota Times*, 29 Dec. 1910.
6 "Fire Department," *The Sarasota Times*, 16 March 1911.
7 "Board of Trade," *The Sarasota Times*, 13 Feb. 1911.
8 "Fire on Main Street," *The Sarasota Times*, 13 April 1911.
9 City of Sarasota, *Meeting of Town Council*, 19 July 1911, Book 1, p.452.

CHAPTER 7. A HUMBLE BEGINNING

1 City of Sarasota, *Ordinance Book No. 1*, 26 Sept. 1911, Ordinance No. 55, p. 163-165.
2 Ibid.
3 Ibid.
4 Ibid.
5 Harry L. Higel to Main Street Merchants, 28 Dec. 1911, Sarasota Fire-Rescue.
6 "Regular Meeting," *The Sarasota Times*, 25 Jan. 1912.
7 "Fire Company Organized," *The Sarasota Times*, 4 April 1912.
8 City of Sarasota, *Minutes of Town Council*, 1 July 1915, Book 2, p. 125.

CHAPTER 8. HENRY BEHRENS

1 *City of Cincinnati and its Resources*, Cincinnati Times Star Co., pp. 75-76, 1891.
2 Certificate of Death, Office of Vital Statistics, Henry George Behrens.
3 "Behrens To Be Missed," *The Herald Tribune*, 14 Dec. 1967.
4 "Historical Society to Display City's First Flag," *The Herald Tribune*, 2 June 1968.
5 Guns and the Good Life, *Guns*, May 1963, p. 28-44.
6 Ibid.
7 "Behrens to be Missed," *The Herald Tribune*, 14 Dec. 1967.
8 Josephine Wensel, interview, Sarasota, 10 Dec. 1989.
9 "Historical Society to Display City's First Flag," *The Herald Tribune*, 2 June 1968.
10 "Behrens to be Missed," *The Herald Tribune*, 14 Dec. 1967.
11 "Historical Society to Display City's First Flag," *The Herald Tribune*, 2 June 1968.
12 Josephine Wensel, interview, Sarasota, 10 Dec. 1989.
13 "Mrs. Henry Behrens," *The Sarasota Times*, 18 Aug. 1910.
14 Marriage License, State of Florida, County of Manatee, Record D, p. 269.
15 Marriage License, State of Florida, County of Manatee, Record E, p. 15.
16 Postcard, Author's Collection.
17 Certificate of Death, Office of Vital Statistics, Henry George Behrens.

CHAPTER 9. THE FIRST FIREHOUSE

1 City of Sarasota, *Meeting of Town Council*, 2 Aug. 1911, p. 455.
2 Harry L. Higel to Town Council, Sarasota Fire-Rescue, 9 Jan. 1912.
3 Hollis P. Bacon to Louise Higel, Sarasota Fire-Rescue, 26 Feb. 1959.
4 Ibid.
5 "A Structure," *The Sarasota Times*, 13 Feb. 1913.
6 "Fish Houses Burned," *The Sarasota Times*, 29 Feb. 1912.
7 Ibid.
8 Ibid.
9 "Blacksmith Shop Burned," *The Sarasota Times*, 15 Aug 1912.
10 Ibid.
11 Ibid.
12 Ibid.

CHAPTER 10. RULES AND REGULATIONS

1 Henry Behrens to Members of Sarasota Fire Department, Sarasota County Dept. of Historical Resources, Behrens File, 15 July 1915.
2 Ibid.
3 City of Sarasota, *Minutes of Town Council*, 24 Jan. 1913, Book 2, p. 31.
4 Ibid.
5 Ibid.
6 Ibid.

CHAPTER 11. THE TURBULENT TEENS

1 " A New Hotel," *The Sarasota Times*, 16 March 1911.
2 "Bay View Hotel Burned," *The Sarasota Times*, 23 Jan. 1913.
3 Ibid.
4 "To Rebuild Bay View," *The Sarosta Times*, 28 Feb. 1913.
5 "Stores Burned on Main Street," *The Sarasota Times*, 8 Jan. 1914.
6 Ibid.
7 Ibid.
8 "H.K. Browning Loses House By Fire, *The Sarasota Times*, 5 March 1914.

CHAPTER 12. HORSEPOWER WITHOUT A HORSE

1 "Council Buy Equipment," *The Sarasota Times*, 14 Jan. 1915.
2 City of Sarasota, *Minutes of Town Council*, 11 Jan. 1915, Book 2.
3 "Equipment for Fighting Fires," *The Sarasota Times*, 29 April 1915.
4 Ibid.
5 Ibid.
6 Ibid.
7 "Sarasota Has Expensive Fire," *The Sarasota Times*, 11 March 1915.
8 Ibid.
9 Ibid.
10 Ibid.
11 Ibid.
12 Ibid.
13 Eula Lastinger, interview, Sarasota, March 26, 1991.
14 "Sarasota Has Expensive Fire," *The Sarasota Times*, 11 March 1915.
15 Ibid.
16 "Equipment for Fighting Fire," *The Sarasota Times*, 29 April 1915.
17 Memo from Henry Behrens to Fire Department Members, Sarasota County Department of Historical Resources, Behrens file, 1 May 1915.
18 Ibid.
19 "Equipment for Fighting Fire," *The Sarasota Times*, 29 April 1915.
20 "Minutes of City Council," *The Sarasota Times*, 20 May 1915.
21 City of Sarasota, *Minutes of Town Council*, 1 July 1915, Book 2, p. 125.
22 Memo from Henry Behrens to Fire Department Members, Sarasota County Department of Historical Resources, Behrens file, 1 May 1915.
23 "Fire Equipment Was Effective," *The Sarasota Times*, 3 June 1915.
24 "Small Fire," *The Sarasota Times*, 27 April 1916.
25 "Minutes of City Council," *The Sarasota Times*, 7 Feb. 1918.
26 City of Sarasota, *Minutes of Town Council*, 19 July 1920, Book 3, p. 450.
27 City of Sarasota, *Minutes of Town Council*, 8 Sept. 1920, p. 473.
28 "Test Report of White," *Henry Behrens Log*, 5 Sept. 1920.
29 Memo from Henry Behrens to Members of Fire Dept., Sarasota County Department of Historical Resources, 5 Sept. 1920.
30 City of Sarasota, *Minutes of Town Council*, 1 Aug. 1921, Book 3, p. 580.
31 City of Sarasota, *Minutes of Town Council*, 21 March 1921, p. 544.

CHAPTER 13. STORMY WEATHER

1 "Council Discharges Fire Chief Behrens," *The Sarasota Times*, 24 Feb. 1921.
2 Ibid.

CHAPTER 13 *(CONTINUED)*

3 City of Sarasota, *Minutes of Town Council*, 21 Feb. 1921, Book 3, p. 534.
4 Ibid.
5 "Council Discharges Fire Chief Behrens," *The Sarasota Times*, 24 Feb. 1921.
6 "An Explanation From Chief of Fire Department," *The Sarasota Times*, 24 Feb. 1921.
7 "Behrens To Be Missed," *The Herald Tribune*, 14 Dec. 1967.
8 "Must Have Permit to Build in Fire Limits," *The Sarasota Times*, 3 March 1921.
9 City of Sarasota, *Minutes of Town Council*, 28 Feb. 1921, Book 3, p. 538.
10 "Must Have Permit to Build In Fire Limits," *The Sarasota Times*, 3 March 1921.
11 "Fire Chief is Given Special Police Powers," *The Sarasota Times*, 14 April 1921.
12 "Must Have Permit to Build in Fire Limits," *The Sarasota Times*, 3 March 1921.
13 Marth, *Yesterday's Sarasota*, p.69.
14 Ibid.
15 City of Sarasota, *Minutes of Town Council*, 23 Jan. 1917, Book 2, p. 249.
16 "Fire Department Moves into Arcade Building," *The Sarasota Times*, 5 May 1921.
17 "Must Have Permit to Build in Fire Limits," *The Sarasota Times*, 3 March 1921.
18 City of Sarasota, *Minutes of Town Council*, 4 April 1921, Book 3, p. 550.
19 "Second Report on Sarasota," *South-Eastern Underwriters Association, Town Report # 172*, 17 April 1929.
20 "New County of Sarasota Takes Its Place As A Political Unit," *The Sarasota County Times*, 30 June 1921.
21 Sarasota County Board of Records, *Minute Book No. 1*, "Senate Bill No. 323, 14 May 1921, pp. 1-4.
22 Miller and Mayfield, Sarasota City Directory for 1921-22 (Florida-Piedmont Directory Co., 1922.
23 "Wilson Brothers See Lots of Changes in Sarasota," *The Sarasota Herald Tribune*, 9 June 1991.
24 National Hurricaine Center, National Weather Service, Coral Gables, Fl.
25 Marth, *Yesterday's Sarasota*, p. 91.
26 "Knowles to Celebrate 25 Years With City," *Florida Fireman*, May 1949, p. 12.

CHAPTER 14. FEAST TO FAMINE

1 *Polk's Sarasota City Directory* 1926 (R.L. Polk and Co., 1925).
2 Marth, *Yesterday's Sarasota*, pp. 102-113.
3 Maitland Knowles, Jr., interview, Englewood, 7 May 1992.
4 Ibid.
5 Miriam Elden/ Knowles, biography of Harry Maitland Knowles, 1962.
6 *Florida Fireman*, May 1949, p. 12.
7 Maitland Knowles, Jr., interview, Englewood, 7 May 1992.
8 Ibid.
9 *Florida Fireman*, May 1949, p. 12.
10 City of Sarasota, Purchase Records, Sarasota Fire-Rescue.
11 City of Sarasota "Report of Fire," 7 Nov. 1952, Sarasota Fire-Rescue.
12 "Peter Pirsch Says City Paid too Much For Fire Apparatus In Buying Truck and Pumper," *This Week in Sarasota*, 16 Dec. 1926., p. 2.
13 Letter from Mayor E. J. Bacon to Peter Pirsch, Sarasota Fire-Rescue, 6 Jan. 1928.
14 Letter from Peter Pirsch to Mayor E. J. Bacon, Sarasota Fire-Rescue, 20 July 1928.
15 "Sarasota's Fire Loss Lowest of Any City in All United States," *This Week in Sarasota*, 16 Dec. 1926.
16 National Hurricaine Center, National Weather Service, Coral Gables, Fl.

CHAPTER 14 *(CONTINUED)*

17 Janet Snyder Matthews, *Sarasota Journey to Centennial*, (Sarasota, Pine Level Press, 1989) pp. 130-131.
18 Letter from Peter Pirsch to Mayor E. J. Bacon, Sarasota Fire-Rescue, 3 Jan. 1927.
19 Proposal for Furnishing Fire Apparatus, City of Sarasota Fire-Rescue, 28 Dec. 1927.
20 City of Sarasota "Report of Fire," City of Sarasota Fire-Rescue, 12 July 1955.
21 "Special Bulletin," *South-Eastern Underwriters Association*, Town Report No. 172, 11 Jan. 1933.
22 James R. Cowsert, Autobiography, Authors Collection, Jan. 1982.
23 Grismer, *The Story of Sarasota*, pp. 244-248.
24 Sarasota County Board of Records, 4 Nov. 1935, Book 6, p. 421.
25 Ibid.
26 "Building's Long Past Ensures Future," *Sarasota Herald Tribune*, 2 Nov. 1987.
27 Ibid.
28 Ibid.
29 *New Sarasota Street Guide*, Sarasota County Department of Historical Resources, 1954 ed., p. 9.
30 Official Program, Florida State Fireman's Twelfth Annual Convention, 26 April 1937.
31 John J. Whelan, Jr., A.I.A., interview, Sarasota, 10 Oct. 1992.
32 "Eight Killed, Two Hurt as Plane From Local Base Crashes," *Sarasota Herald Tribune*, 12 June 1942.
33 "Fireman Need Trousers," *Sarasota Herald Tribune*, 8 Dec. 1942.
34 Grismer, *The Story of Sarasota*, pp. 235-238.
35 "Knowles to Celebrate 25 Years with City," *Florida Fireman*, May 1949, p. 12.
36 "Resolution," City Commission, 7 April 1952.

CHAPTER 15. POPS

1 "Knowles to Celebrate 25 Years With City," *Florida Fireman*, May 1949, p. 12.
2 James R. Cowsert, Autobiography, Authors Collection, Jan. 1982.
3 Ibid.
4 Ibid.
5 "Fire Chief Ends 41 1/2 Year Career," *Sarasota Herald Tribune*.
6 Maitland Knowles, Jr., interview, Englewood, 7 May 1992.
7 Ibid.
8 Mrs. James Cowsert, interview, Sarasota, 1988.
9 "Living Quarters," *Sarasota Herald Tribune*, 3 Nov. 1955.
10 "Sarasota Department Moves Into New Station," *Florida Fireman*, March 1960, p. 8.
11 "Central Station Move More Than Relocation," *The News*, 31 Jan 1960, p. 9.
12 Roger V. Flory, *Sarasota Visitors Guide* (Roger V. Flory, 1958) p. 52.
13 "Central Station Move More than Relocation," *The News*, 31 Jan. 1960, p. 9.
14 Ibid.
15 James R. Cowsert, Autobiography, Authors Collection, Jan 1982.
16 M.S.A. Product Literature.
17 "Modernization Listed Top Advancement By Cowsert," *Sarasota Herald Tribune*, 5 June 1966.
18 "Fire Chief Ends 41½ Year Career," *Sarasota Herald Tribune*.

CHAPTER 16. BACKDRAFT

1 Harold Stinchcomb, interview, Sarasota, 6 June 1991.
2 Ibid.
3 "Sarasota Fire Station Open House Set Sunday," *The Tampa Tribune*, 4 June 1971.
4 Harold Stinchcomb, interview, Sarasota, 6 June 1991.
5 Ibid.
6 Jim Olson, interview, Sarasota, 7 May 1991.
7 City of Sarasota, Alarm and Fire Record, Alarm No. 3080, 1 April 1979.

CHAPTER 16 (CONTINUED)

8 Jim Olson, interview, Sarasota, 7 May 1991.
9 City of Sarasota, Alarm and Fire Record, Alarm No. 3080, 1 April 1979.
10 Ibid.
11 Jim Olson, interview, Sarasota, 7 May 1991.
12 Ibid.
13 City of Sarasota, Alarm and Fire Record, Alarm No. 3080, 1 April 1979.
14 Ibid.
15 Charlena Jenkins, interview, Sarasota, 6 Feb. 1993.
16 *Program: Opening Ceremony*, Sarasota Fire-Rescue, 1988.
17 Letter from H.R. Stinchcomb to Mr. David Sollenberger, Sarasota Fire-Rescue, 7 April 1988.
18 Thomas Fields, interview, Sarasota, 4 July 1992.

CHAPTER 17. FROM A DISTANCE: COMMUNICATIONS IN THE FIRE DEPARTMENT

1 Memo from Henry Behrens to Members of Sarasota Fire Department, Sarasota Fire-Rescue, 28 July 1915.
2 Ibid.
3 "Bay View House Fire," *The Sarasota Times*, 10 Feb. 1910.
4 "Fire Alarm Should Be Given Promptly," *The Sarasota Times*, 1 July 1915.
5 *Sarasota Street Guide and Informant*, (Sarasota, Star Printing, 1942).
6 City of Sarasota, *Minutes of Town Council*, 1 July 1915, Book 2, p. 125.
7 "City Will Abandon Use of 30-Year Fire Horn," *Sarasota Herald Tribune*, 6 Dec. 1955.
8 "New Fire Alarm Has Been Installed By City," *The Sarasota Times*, 24 June 1920.
9 Elbert E. Friend, Communications Supervisor/ Retired, interview, Sarasota, 16 Sept. 1992.
10 Gamewell Fire Alarm File, Sarasota Fire-Rescue.
11 Ibid.
12 Elbert E. Friend, Communications Supervisor/ Retired, interview, Sarasota, 16 Sept. 1992.
13 Ibid.
14 Gamewell Fire Alarm File, Sarasota Fire-Rescue.
15 "New Fire Alarm Has Been Installed By City," *The Sarasota Times*, 24 June 1920.
16 "City Will Abandon Use of 30-Year Fire Horn," *Sarasota Herald Tribune*, 6 Dec. 1955.
17 Ibid.
18 Elbert E. Friend, Communications Supervisor/ Retired, interview, Sarasota, 16 Sept. 1992.
19 "Working For You 24 Hours A Day," *Sarasota Herald Tribune*.
20 Elbert E. Friend, Communications Supervisor/ Retired, interview, Sarasota, 16 Sept. 1992.
21 Ibid.
22 Ibid.
23 "Sarasota Installs Florida's First Radio-Telemetry Fire Alarm System," *Florida Fireman*, Dec. 1971, p. 21.
24 Elbert E. Friend, Communications Supervisor/ Retired, interview, Sarasota, 16 Sept. 1992.
25 Gamewell Fire Alarm File, Sarasota Fire-Rescue.
26 "Sarasota Installs Florida's First Radio-Telemetry Fire Alarm System," *Florida Fireman*, Dec. 1971, p. 21.
27 Elbert E. Friend, Communications Supervisor/ Retired, interview, Sarasota, 16 Sept. 1992.
28 Ibid.
29 "Sarasota Installs Florida's First Radio-Telemetry Fire Alarm System," *Florida Fireman*, Dec. 1971, p. 21.
30 Elbert E. Friend, Communications Supervisor/ Retired, interview, Sarasota, 16 Sept. 1992.
31 "Fire Dispatcher Must Keep His Cool When The Emergency Gets Hot," *Sarasota Herald Tribune*, 9 Feb. 1973.
32 Elbert E. Friend, Communications Supervisor/ Retired, interview, Sarasota, 16 Sept. 1992.

CHAPTER 17 (CONTINUED)

33 "Computerized Dispatch System Saves Valuable Seconds Answering Fire Calls," *Sarasota Journal*, 10 Dec. 1981.
34 Elbert E. Friend, Communications Supervisor/ Retired, interview, Sarasota, 16 Sept. 1992.
35 "New Dispatching System Will Centralize North Sarasota County's Fire Stations," *Sarasota Herald Tribune*, 4 Sept. 1984.
36 Dispatch Records, Sarasota Fire-Rescue.
37 Dispatch Records, Sarasota Fire-Rescue, 1991-93.
38 Ibid.

CHAPTER 18. A SECOND CHANCE: EMERGENCY MEDICAL SERVICES

1 Grismer, *The Story of Sarasota*, p. 39.
2 A.J. Petellat, telephone interview, 7 Feb. 1993.
3 "Contribute $150. to Fire Dept. Iron Lung Fund," *Minutes of Sarasota County Commission*, 3 April 1944, Book 10, p. 378.
4 E + J Resuscitator, product literature.
5 Robert Lamb, interview, Sarasota, 1993.
6 Dale Oswalt, interview, Sarasota, 1993.
7 Don Grant, interview, Sarasota, 1993.
8 "Motel, Hotels on Lido Buy Resuscitator," *Sarasota Herald Tribune*, 5 June 1958.
9 Don Grant, interview, Sarasota, 1993.
10 "Fully Equipped First Aid Truck In Operation By City Fire Department," *Sarasota Herald Tribune*, 30 Nov. 1948.
11 Ibid.
12 "Defends Ambulance Service," *Sarasota Herald Tribune*, 26 Nov. 1972.
13 Ibid.
14 "Notice," *Sarasota Herald Tribune*, 15 April 1973.
15 "Ambulance Issue Heats Up," *Sarasota Journal*, 1 Dec. 1972.
16 Ibid.
17 "Sarasotan's Tune In on Emergency," *Sarasota Herald Tribune*, 28 Jan 1973.
18 "City Ambulances Due By April 1," *Sarasota Journal*, 20 March 1971.
19 "Ambulance Service Question Revised," *Sarasota Journal*, Aug. 1972.
20 "Fire Department's Ambulance Success," *Sarasota Herald Tribune*, 29 April 1973.
21 "Firemen Receive Certificates," *Sarasota Herald Tribune*, 19 Aug. 1972.
22 Linda Schlumbrecht, Md., interview, Sarasota, 1972.
23 Don Grant, interview, Sarasota, 1993.
24 Ibid.
25 "Rescue Squad Telemetry Equipment Use Delayed," *Sarasota Journal*, 29 Aug. 1973.
26 "New Rescue Techniques Save Victim," *Sarasota Herald Tribune*, 29 Jan. 1974.
27 Don Grant, interview, Sarasota, 1993.
28 Dispatch Records, Sarasota Fire-Rescue, 1992.

CHAPTER 19. THE GOLDEN HOUR: TRAUMA CARE

1 Jon Franklin and Alan Doelp, <u>Shock-Trauma</u>, (New York: St. Martins Press, 1980), pp. 1-8.

CHAPTER 20. MOVING FORWARD TOGETHER

1 Personnel Records, City of Sarasota.
2 *International Firefighter*, (AFL-CIO/CLC, Nov-Dec 1992), vol. 74, No. 6, pp. 13-15.
3 *This Week in Sarasota Scrapbook*, April 8, 1926, p. 15.

CHAPTER 21. EXCELLENCE AND PRIDE

1 Julius E. Halas, interview, Sarasota, 1993.
2 Greg Faegans, Director, Sarasota County Department of Emergency Management, interview, Sarasota, 1993.
3 Ibid.

SELECT BIBLIOGRAPHY

BOOKS

B & B ASSOCIATES. *New Sarasota Street Guide*, 1954.

BOARD OF TRADE. *Information Relative to Sarasota*. Sarasota, Florida.

BRIGGS, CHARLIE. *One Hundred Years Ago: Old-Time Sarasota*. Sarasota: Jere Parker, 1986.

BROWN, CANTER, JR. *Florida's Peace River Frontier*. Gainesville: University of Central Florida Press, 1991.

BROWNING, ALEX. *Browning Family Manuscript*. Sarasota: Sarasota County Department of Historical Resources, 1932.

BURNETT, GENE M. *Florida's Past*. Englewood: Pineapple Press, Inc., 1986.

FLORY, ROGER V. *Sarasota Visitors Guide*. Sarasota: Roger V. Flory, 1958.

FRANKLIN, JON AND DOELP, ALAN. *Shock-Trauma*. New York: St. Martins Press, 1980.

GRISMER, KARL H. *The Story of Sarasota*. 2d ed. Sarasota: M.E. Russell, 1946. Reprint. Paschal and Paschal Publishers, Inc., 1977.

LANDERS, EDNA MOSELY. *Biography of Mary Wyatt Whitaker*. Sarasota: Sarasota County Department of Historical Resources.

MARTH, DEL. *Yesterday's Sarasota: Including Sarasota County*. 1st paperback ed. Sarasota: Lindsay Curtis Publishing Co., 1977.

MATTHEWS, JANET SNYDER. *Sarasota: Journey to Centennial*. Sarasota: Pine Level Press, Inc., 1989.

MCDUFFEE, LILLIE B. *The Lures of Manatee*. 2nd ed. Bradenton: A.K. Whitaker and Manatee County Historical Society, 1961.

MILLER AND MAYFIELD. *Sarasota City Directory for 1921-22*. Florida: Piedmont Directory Co., 1922.

Minute Book of Sarasota County, Sarasota County Board of Records.

Minutes of Town Council, Sarasota Florida.

Ordinances of the Town of Sarasota, Sarasota Florida.

PASCHAL, GUY. *A Vivid History of Sarasota*.

POLK, R.L. *Polk's Sarasota City Directory 1926*. R.L. Polk and Co., 1925.

STAR PRINTING CO. *Sarasota Street Guide and Informant*. Sarasota: Star Printing Co., 1942.

TOWN COUNCIL. *Ordinances of the Town of Sarasota*. Original Document. Sarasota: Town Council, 1903.

TRICEBOCH, KENNETH F. *Explore Sarasota and Vicinity*. 8th ed., 1992.

UNKNOWN. *The City of Cincinnatti and Its Resources*. Cincinnatti: Cincinnatti Times Star Co., 1891.

WHITAKER, A.K. *One Man's Family*. Sarasota: Sarasota County Department of Historical Resources, 1969.

NEWSPAPERS AND MAGAZINES

Florida Fireman

Guns

Harper's Weekly

International Firefighter

Manatee River Journal

Sarasota Herald

Sarasota Herald Tribune

Sarasota Journal

This Week in Sarasota

Sarasota Times

The Bradenton Herald

The News-Sarasota

The Tampa Tribune

OTHER

NATIONAL HURRICAINE CENTER, National Weather Service, Coral Gables, Florida.